Colors!

Colors!

Stories of the Kingdom

JOHN R. AURELIO

CROSSROAD • NEW YORK

1993

The Crossroad Publishing Company
370 Lexington Avenue, New York, NY 10017

Copyright © 1993 by John R. Aurelio

Printed in the United States of America

Library of Congress Cataloging-in-Publication Data
Aurelio, John.
    Colors : stories of the Kingdom / by John R. Aurelio.
        p. cm.
    ISBN 0-8245-1361-4
    1. Christian stories, American. 2. Fairy tales—United States.
I. Title.
PS3551.U76C65 1993
813'.54—dc20
                                                    93-15750
                                                        CIP

This book is affectionately dedicated to all the wonderful people
who have borne with me and my stories over the years
at social gatherings, in class, and at conferences.
Your love and encouragement over the years
have colored my life and my stories.

Contents

Preface

MYOPIA

Whites see a white world.
Blacks see a black one.
Hispanics see a brown world,
and Indians see a red one.

French see a Gallic world.
Germans see a Teutonic one.
Philosophers see a heavenly world,
and farmers see an earthy one.

Rich see a bright world.
Poor see a gloomy one.
Intellectuals see a complex world,
and retarded see a simple one.

Men see a man's world.
Women see a woman's one.
Adults see a troubled world,
and youth see a fun one.

Haves see a full world.
Have-nots see an empty one.
Muslims see a Moslem world,
and Christians see a divided one.

Doctors see a sick world.
Lawyers see a litigious one.
Believers see a sinful world,
and atheists see a better one.

Cities see an urban world.
States see a stately one.
Optimists see a hopeful world,
and pessimists don't even see one.

I see a myopic world,
and God sees only — *one.*

Somewhere in the scriptures it says that God says "one" and we hear "two." We are forever analyzing and interpreting. But I stand between a publisher who says let the stories stand for themselves and a number of people who ask me to explain them or tell how to use them. As a sort of compromise I have used the Aesopian technique of putting a moral at the end of many of them.

I have also included as fillers at the end of some of the stories pithy little lessons life has taught me. At times I can be brief.

The world cannot live without myths any more than people can. A myth is not a fiction but a belief embodied in a story that helps to make reality worth living. Science and reason provide the seed and myth provides the edible fruit. No more than a pill will ever supplant steak and potatoes will facts ever do away with myths. New facts simply create new myths. In the end the world belongs to the storytellers.

Finally, I would like to add a special word of thanks to Michael Leach, Gene Gollogly, and Sister Mary Margaret Doorley of Crossroad for their never-ending support.

The Little Angel with No Wings

ONCE UPON A TIME, up in heaven, there was a little angel who discovered that he had no wings. His name was Johnny — Johnny Angel. Johnny didn't know why he didn't have wings, so he asked one of the other angels.

"You'd better ask an archangel," he said. "Archangels know just about everything."

Johnny was a little nervous about seeing an archangel. After all archangels are principal angels, and they're very busy besides being smart and important. But he wanted wings like the other angels, and he just had to know why he didn't have any.

When he entered the principal archangel's office he stood in front of his desk meek as a little bird not uttering a peep. The principal archangel bent his head down and looked over his glasses at Johnny. "Cat got your tongue!" he barked. "Speak up, boy, speak up. What's on your mind?"

"I don't have wings," Johnny blurted out.

"That's right."

"The other angels have wings," he said.

"That's right."

"Some have big, white, puffy wings."

"That's right."

"Some have pretty, colored wings."

"That's right."

"Some angels have wings that beat so fast you can hardly see them."

"That's right."

"I don't have any wings," Johnny said again.

"That's right," the principal archangel said again.

"Why?"

"Because you have to earn your wings," he said.

"What do I have to do?"

"Go see Mortimer at the wing warehouse," he said, and then got busy at his desk again. Johnny turned to leave when the principal archangel stopped him.

"Remember, whatever you do, you must never let a human see you. People are not supposed to see us. If one of them does you will never get your wings."

Johnny was so shocked by this warning he had to repeat it just to make sure. "You mean, if anybody on earth sees me I won't get my wings?"

"That's right," he said, and the interview was over.

When Johnny got to the wing warehouse he was amazed at all the different kinds of wings there were. They came in all sizes and colors and shapes. "Why are there so many different kinds?" he asked Mortimer the Wing Angel.

"It depends on what you want to do."

"I don't know yet what I want to do," Johnny said.

"Then pick a pair and I'll tell you."

Johnny picked a pair with all colors.

"Good choice," Mortimer Angel said. "Those are our rainbow wings. Now what you do is go and find some other angels with rainbow wings and whenever the world needs a rainbow, you go with them and make a rainbow. But remember. You must never let people get close enough to see your face or you'll never get your own wings."

This is going to be fun, Johnny thought. He no sooner found a group of rainbow angels that they got called to earth to make a rainbow. It had just finished raining over a forest, and they made a beautiful rainbow over a lake. When people came out to look at them, Johnny got frightened and almost flew away. The other angels laughed and told him not to worry because they were too far away for the people to see their faces. "This is wonderful," Johnny said. "I like being a rainbow angel."

He was just beginning to enjoy shining in the sun with all the people admiring him, when the others told him it was time to go.

"Why?" Johnny asked.

"We only work after a rain when the sun comes out to shine. But just for a short time," they told him as they returned to heaven.

Johnny loved his pretty colored wings and enjoyed being a rainbow with the other angels but he wanted to do more. So when the rainbow angels, weren't busy he went off by himself looking for something to do. He discovered that he could show up almost anytime there was a waterfall or a mist and the sun was shining. However, if the sun didn't shine his pretty colored wings wouldn't light up.

Soon Johnny began showing up by himself at little waterfalls and babbling brooks. But this got to be a little dangerous because children would come running up to him unexpectedly to get a good look at him, and he would have to disappear quickly. He had a few really close calls. He decided to stick with the really big rainbows that were far enough away to stay out of trouble.

After a while, though, he got bored and went back to the wing warehouse.

"What's up?" Mortimer asked.

"The rainbow wings are nice," Johnny said, "but I want to try something else."

"I understand," Mortimer said. "How about these nice big, fluffy, white ones. They're a very popular model."

Even though they were very big, almost bigger than he was,

Johnny was surprised at how light they were. "What do I do with these wings?" he asked.

"Those are our cloud wings," Mortimer said. "Go join some other cloud angels and you'll have plenty to do."

It wasn't hard to find cloud angels at all. There were a lot more of them than rainbow angels. Johnny joined a group of them and went to work immediately.

It was wonderful being a cloud angel. Johnny got to drift lazily over so many different and interesting places. He moved over mountains and forests, over cities and valleys. There were just so many exciting things to see.

And that was the problem. They were floating too high up for him to see things up close. So, every once in a while he would break away from a group of cloud angels and go off by himself. He was careful not to get too close to cities where there were so many people that someone might just see his face. He explored mostly woods and mountains by himself. Yet even here it was dangerous because one day a group of mountain climbers suddenly came around a rock and almost walked right into him. A lucky breeze blew him away just in the nick of time. He decided that he'd better stay with the cloud angels up in the sky where it was safe.

After a while, Johnny got bored with this too. He went back to the wing warehouse.

"Still haven't found the right pair, eh?" Mortimer said.

"Oh, the cloud wings were all right, but I didn't get around enough to make me happy," Johnny sighed.

"Why didn't you tell me you want to get around a lot," Mortimer laughed. "I've got just the wings for you, my boy." He gave Johnny a curious looking pair of rather short wings.

"They're kinda short," Johnny said, trying not to sound disappointed.

"That's because they're our racing model."

"Racing model? What do you do with them?"

"These are our wind wings. You make wind with them. Just try them. I'm sure you'll like them."

When Johnny put them on, they began to beat so fast he could hardly remain in one spot. He did all he could to keep himself from spinning like a windmill.

"Now go find some other wind angels and go to it, boy."

Johnny was off like a whirlwind. Now this was exciting. He and some other wind angels blew around everywhere. He loved scattering fallen leaves in front of him, sending kites soaring and twirling in the sky, blowing sailboats across a lake, and whistling through trees and mountain caves. He wasn't even afraid to get close to people because he moved so fast there was no danger of them seeing him. He would blow across their faces and watch them turn red, and when he felt especially mischievous he would tousle their hair and laugh at how funny he made them look. It was wonderful being a wind angel. These were the wings for him.

One day as it was getting on toward evening Johnny thought he would rustle around a forest for a while before going back to heaven for a rest. He had chased a few rabbits into their burrows and ruffled the feathers of an owl when he heard the barking of a dog not too far away. The dog was hot on the scent of a forest creature. Johnny decided to have a little fun with the animal, so he blew into the dog's nose. The dog sneezed. When he tried to pick up the scent again, Johnny blew into his nose again. The dog sneezed again. After a few more times and a few more sneezes the dog lost the scent and just sat down. By now it was dark so the dog curled up and went to sleep.

Since it was dark and there was no more mischief he could do here, Johnny decided to head home. As he was flying just above the tree tops he heard the faint cry of a boy weeping somewhere in the forest below him. He was curious that a boy should be out in the woods so late at night, so he decided to take a careful look. Even though it was pitch black angels have no trouble seeing in the dark. He found the boy seated beneath a big oak tree sobbing uncontrollably. Johnny didn't know what to do. He couldn't just leave this boy here all alone, all night. But how could he help him? What if the boy were to see his face?

He finally decided that the boy couldn't see him in the dark anyway, so he spoke to him.

"What's the matter boy? Are you lost?"

The boy was so startled to hear his voice that he stopped crying. "Who are you?" he asked, not knowing where to look.

"I was just passing through the woods when I heard you crying," Johnny said. "What's the matter?" he asked again a little nervous since this was the first time he had ever spoken to a human.

The boy started sobbing again. "I was playing in the woods with my dog," he cried, "and then he disappeared. He always comes back to me but this time he didn't. I don't know my way out of the woods without him."

Oh, dear! Johnny thought. I was just having a little fun and now I caused this problem. It's all my fault. What am I going to do?

"You're dog is probably just sleeping somewhere. Why don't you just go to sleep yourself? I'm sure he'll find you in the morning and lead you home."

"I can't," the boy sobbed." I don't want to be all alone in the dark. Will you help me?"

How could he help him out of the forest? What if somebody were to see him? But how could he not help him out. After all, it was his fault the boy was in this trouble. He would have to chance it.

"I'll help you," he said. "Take my hand."

"I can't see you," the boy said.

Johnny reached out and took the boy by the hand. "Now I'll lead you out. Just follow me."

Johnny could see in the dark, but the boy couldn't, and he immediately stumbled and fell.

"I can't," the boy started crying all over again. "I can't see anything." The tears came in a torrent now. "I want my dog. I want to go home," he cried over and over again.

Johnny was at a loss over what to do. "Dear God, please, help me," Johnny prayed.

At that moment he saw a firefly flicker nearby. "I know," Johnny shouted. "Don't worry," he said to the boy. "I'll only be gone for a few moments and then I'll help you find your dog and get out of the woods."

Before the boy could say a word Johnny was gone quick as a breeze. In just a few moments he had collected in his hands a whole swarm of fireflies. The glow of them shone right through his hands so that they lit up the area around him like a lamp.

But he'll see my face, Johnny thought and pondered. The delay was just long enough for the boy to start crying all over again.

"If I'm going to do it, I'd better do it now," he said and stepped out from behind the trees. The boy looked directly at him. Then he looked at the light in his hands. "How did you do that?" he asked.

"Never mind," Johnny said. "Let's go find your dog."

Leading the way with his lighted hands, Johnny took the boy to the place where his dog lay sleeping. The boy screamed with delight over finding his dog. Then Johnny led the two of them slowly through the dark forest.

As they neared the edge of the woods they could hear the shouts of people calling out.

"I'm over here, Daddy. I'm over here, Mommy," the boy cried back.

"You'll be all right now," Johnny said. Before the boy could thank him, he set the fireflies free and it became dark again. But when he went to beat his wings to leave, they were gone. His wings were really gone. It happened just like Mortimer and the archangel had warned him. The boy had seen his face and Johnny lost his wings just like they said he would. Johnny hid behind a tree not knowing what to do.

The boy's parents came and led him away by lamp light. The boy was telling them about the mysterious stranger who helped him through the forest. Just before they were out of earshot, Johnny heard the boy ask his parents, "Who was he?"

"I don't know," his mother said, "but if you ask me, I'd say he was an angel."

Johnny walked through the forest almost the whole night wondering what was to become of him. Just as the sun rose Mortimer came to get him. He took him to the principal archangel.

"I guess you blew it," the archangel said, "if you'll pardon my pun."

"I guess I did," Johnny answered sheepishly.

"You were a rainbow," the archangel said peering down at him over his glasses.

"That's right," Johnny said.

"You were a cloud."

"That's right."

"You were a wind."

"That's right."

"Your face was seen."

"That's right."

"Why?"

"Because it was my fault and I had to help him."

"How did you help him?"

"I caught fireflies and made a lamp out of my hands because he was afraid of the dark."

"Clever idea. But it cost you your wings."

"I know. What do I do now?"

"I don't know. This has never happened before. Wait here while I consult about this."

When the archangel returned he was smiling. This made Johnny feel better, but he was still curious about what they were going to do with him.

"Well, we've got a solution. Because you risked your wings for the love of a child who was afraid of the dark, it has been decided that from now on the night sky will no longer be dark. God will put up stars. Lots of them. Millions and billions of them so that the night will not be so dark and frightening to children anymore. And because of you we are starting a whole new order of angels . . ." here he paused making the suspense unbearable. "They will be called star angels and you, Johnny Angel, will be the first one."

Johnny was so happy with the news that he began to beam so brightly he filled the heavens with a brilliant light.

"At night," the archangel said. "AT NIGHT!"

Then, as the archangel left to go about his business, he looked over his shoulder and said, "Oh, I almost forgot. I'm also supposed to tell you that God has a very special job for you on Christmas night."

So now when children all over the world are afraid at night, all they have to do is look up into the sky and see Johnny and all the star angels waving at them.

But from a distance. So that you can't see their faces.

~ 2 ~

Watermelon Seeds

WHEN GOD FINISHED CREATING the heavens and the earth, everything was beautiful and orderly. The days passed in regular progression; the earth moved to the rhythm of the seasons; the trees and plants bore their fruit; and goodness abounded.

Then one day Father Adam sighed a deep and heavy sigh before the Lord.

"What is it that is troubling you, man?" he asked. "Are not the heavens and the earth a wonder of symmetry and beauty that please the eye and delight the soul?"

"I suppose," Adam sighed again.

"Then what is bothering you?" He asked again.

"I'm bored," he sighed.

"Why are you bored?" asked the Lord.

"Because there's no excitement here. Everything is so orderly there are no surprises. Take the sun, for instance. Every day the sun comes up and every night the sun goes down. That's boring. For a while the moon excited me because it changed its face. But now I know that it changes its face in the same way every month and that's boring. The tides come in and the tides go out, the seasons come and go with monotonous regularity. Even the plants are boring. Take this watermelon, for instance." Adam pointed to a perfectly shaped watermelon lying at his feet. "Now I must admit that I do love watermelons. But when I have finished eating it, I will plant its seed and new watermelons will grow."

"What's wrong with that?" the Lord asked.

"It's boring. That's what's wrong with it."

"How would you do it?" the Lord asked patiently.

"How about if I were to plant watermelon seeds and have them grow into apple trees. Now that would be different and exciting."

"Then you would get tired of them growing into apple trees," the Lord said, trying desperately to follow Adam's logic.

"You're too logical," Adam exclaimed, anticipating the Lord's reaction. "The next time you planted them, they might grow into roses. Then maybe oranges. Each time it would be different. Each time it would be a surprise."

"But you'd never know," God reasoned, "You could never plan."

"There! You're at it again," complained Adam. "That's exactly what I mean. With you everything is so predictable. That's what makes everything boring."

"How would you have it?"

"If I were to have my way I would have it so that nothing is predictable. Everything would be a surprise."

"Then have it your way," said the Lord, and the sun immediately set.

The night lasted at least eight days, if you could reckon time according to days. However, since there was no regularity of days, or even of minutes, for the length of minutes changed too, there was no way of telling exactly how long it lasted. The only thing Adam felt sure of was that the next time it would not last the same amount of time. But then he couldn't really be sure of that either since certainty is not possible without regularity and regularity was a bore and boredom was forbidden. Therefore, nothing was certain anymore.

When the sun shone again, it began to snow. Adam laughed. It was delightful. He gathered clothes to bundle himself up against the cold. No sooner had he finished when the snow melted and it became torridly hot. He shed his heavy clothes immediately and decided to refresh himself by bathing in a lake.

Fortunately, he chose not to dive in or he might have hurt himself since the water was rock hard. Or maybe he wouldn't have hurt himself since he could no longer be sure of anything. He discovered that soon enough when the water in the middle of the lake was liquid and he fell through. He sank to the bottom like a rock. Holding his breath he swam back to the top but couldn't break through the hard surface. There was nothing more he could do. He was certain to drown. But nothing was certain anymore. When he could no longer hold his breath, he breathed in water. To his utter amazement, he discovered that he could breathe underwater.

This was a new wonder, indeed. He walked and swam under the water exploring everything, yet never experiencing the same thing twice. When he grew hungry, he emerged and went off looking for food.

There is no telling of all the strange and remarkable things he encountered while in this pursuit, except to say that when he was finished he had an uncontrollable craving for watermelon. He searched high and low, far and wide, but could not find one. The longer he searched the more of an obsession it became. Time changed all around him, plants grew and disappeared, clouds fell and worms flew. But none of this meant anything to him. He couldn't stand it any longer. Finally, he called to God.

"Yes, Adam."

"I must have some watermelon."

"Go plant some seeds," the Lord said.

"You know I can't," he sulked.

"Oh, but you can. You just can't plant watermelon seeds if you want watermelons. But, then again, you just might get watermelons from watermelon seeds. It's just that you can't be certain, you understand."

"I give," Adam conceded.

"Where were you, Man, when I created the universe, and set the stars in their places and fixed the boundaries of things. Have you done better?"

"No," Adam mumbled.

"Then leave the heavens and the earth to me." Having said that everything returned to normal. And the Lord left.

Adam sighed. He looked around furtively and whispered under his breath, "It's still boring."

~ Moral ~

What you sow is what you reap.

 *Limerick*

There was a young man from Poughkeepsie
Who heard of a drink that makes you tipsy.
To get some he traveled a year and a day
Only to find to his great dismay
That the damn stuff was made in Poughkeepsie.

The Rainbow Rose

ONCE UPON A TIME, the queen of France gave birth to a beautiful baby boy. The next day, the king called in the royal gardener and told him of a very special plan he had for the prince.

"A wise king," he said, "must always plan ahead for the future. One day the prince will inherit the kingdom and himself become the king of France. I will choose for him a most beautiful bride to be his queen. What I wish for her to honor the occasion is a magnificently beautiful flower, one more beautiful than any other flower in the realm. You, my trusted gardener, must develop such a flower as to do her justice and honor me."

The royal gardener began at once in obedience to the king's wish. He decided on the rose since it is the most regal of all the flowers. Over the months and years he experimented, taking the pollen from one, mixing it with another, and creating all manner of interesting blooms. He even mixed it with other blossoms to develop different shapes and colors. As beautiful as many of them were, they were never quite good enough to please him. But he never gave up, not even when the good king died in battle.

The young regent did not marry for a long time, so the gardener continued with his work, growing old and feeble in the process. At last, the good news came. The young king had chosen a bride and the date for the royal wedding was set. It came none too soon, for the old gardener had finally achieved his masterpiece. It was a rose that rivaled the very heavens with its beauty. In fact, it was the heavens that gave it its beauty, for it was so delicate and fine, like lace porcelain, that it mirrored all the colors that surrounded it. Though it sat in the middle of the garden surrounded by myriad other blossoms, it outshone them like a queen among peasants. He had done the old king honor and himself proud.

On the day of the wedding a magnificent rainbow arched across the early morning sky. All its wonderful colors were reflected in the prize rose. Since he had created it, it was the gardener's right to name it. He called it the Rainbow Rose. He hobbled back to his cottage and sat there waiting for the new queen to claim her prize.

While the sun was still high in the heavens and the rose gleamed with awesome beauty, the newlyweds entered the royal garden. The old gardener was not surprised to see that they made their way immediately to the regal bloom. With her back to the gardener the queen reached down and picked the blossom. The old man smiled. "A royal rose for a royal beauty," he sighed.

When the queen turned and faced him, he saw that the rose she held to her face was not the Rainbow Rose at all but just a common, ordinary red rose. He was shocked at first. Then angry. How could she? How could she pass over the royal bloom he had labored for many long years to develop? How could she discredit him and dishonor the dead king?

He struggled to his feet. Anger blazed in his heart as he stumbled toward her. He could not restrain himself. He must know why she rejected the Rainbow Rose. He called out to her. "My lady!" The queen looked up at him still holding that damnable rose to her face. With fire in his eyes, he looked into hers.

At once he knew. She had discovered the prize rose's only flaw. It had no scent. The queen was blind.

~ Moral ~

God does not judge by appearances.

 ### Comparisons

People who can't look at life
without comparing everything to themselves
can never appreciate life for its own sake.

 ### Potatoes

Do you eat potatoes
and then once you've eaten them
never have them again?
That's why we serve them
mashed, boiled, fried, scalloped, and au gratin.

~ 4 ~

Stones

THERE WAS A BOY who lived by the sea. Each day he would go off to school walking along the shore, and then return by the same route.

One day a pretty colored stone sparkling in the sunlight caught his eye. He reached down and picked it up. After admiring it for a while, he decided to keep it, so he put it into his pocket. On his way back from school he kept his eyes peeled for the possibility of finding more such pretty stones. When he found a few, he put them too in his pocket and took them home.

Each day the sea would wash up new stones upon the shore and each day he found more colored stones to take along with him. It became a daily ritual.

Even when the boy became a man the routine did not change. He would gather stones on his way to and from work and carry them with him.

One day, after he had gathered a truly excessive number of stones, so that all his pockets were bulging and the weight of them was oppressive, he noticed an old man watching him.

"What are you doing?" the old man asked.

"Gathering stones," he replied.

"Why?"

"I really don't know. It's just a habit, I suppose."

"Does it please you?"

"It did once."

Without saying another word, the old man came over to him and began emptying his pockets. When the man saw what he was doing he joined in until he had no more stones in any of his pockets. He felt relieved — then exhilarated — as if a heavy burden had been lifted from him. He rejoiced all the way home.

The next day as he walked along the shore he began to gather stones once more.

"What are you doing?" the old man asked.

"Gathering stones again," the man replied.

"Why?"

"I guess gathering stones has become a part of me," he answered. "What else would I do as I pass along this way?"

"Gather flowers."

The man saw that there were also flowers along the shore.

From that day on the man gathered flowers instead of stones. Besides, they were easier to carry and more pleasant to give away.

~ Moral ~

Good works are lighter than sins.

 Love

"God is love" defines God.
The reverse defines us.

The Jigsaw Puzzle

ONCE UPON A TIME there was a piece of a jigsaw puzzle. It didn't know that it was a piece of a jigsaw puzzle. It just knew that it was there and it was rather nice to be there. It lived among other pieces of a jigsaw puzzle but didn't know that they were pieces of a puzzle. As a matter of fact, they didn't know that they were either. They just lived together in the same place all jumbled up.

This puzzle piece lived fairly well all by itself as did all the other pieces. They all did their own thing every day. Each one ate its own food, drank its own drink, did its own work, enjoyed its own peace, and slept its own sleep.

Only occasionally did this piece wonder why it was different from all the other pieces that surrounded it; why it preferred to eat some foods and not others; do some types of work, but not others; why it felt good among some pieces and just a bit uncomfortable among others. But it wondered only occasionally. The questions really didn't affect its life very much.

Then one day a very strange thing happened. For some unexplainable reason, it was intensely drawn to another puzzle piece. It was as if some magnet were drawing it against its own will. Perhaps it was because it was green like itself. But it had seen other green pieces and wasn't particularly drawn to them. This time it was just too much.

When the two pieces joined together it felt indescribably good. It was a whole new experience for both of them. Immediately, they felt as if this was what was meant to be from the beginning. They fit. When other pieces of the puzzle saw them together, they began pairing off — the blues with the blue, the browns with the brown, the square with the square, and so on. Some pieces chose to leave well enough alone and stay just the way they were. Others could find no match. Still others had given up trying. Those who did connect felt more fulfilled than they did before. It seemed that suddenly there was a flurry of frantic activity.

At one point two pairs of pieces discovered that they fit together. Then another two tried it and fit. Soon others were trying it. Before long, pieces were moving around everywhere. While it seemed all jumbled up with single pieces joining triplets and doubles becoming quartets and then octets, it somehow all made sense.

In the midst of all this hustle and bustle our original puzzle piece shouted out, "Where will it all end?"

Everything quite dramatically stopped. What with all the mixing and matching and pairing, no one had hitherto given any thought to how it would all end. Yes, how would it all end? Where would it all end? When would it all end?

All the pieces began offering their own ideas. Some believed one thing, others another. They began separating themselves from each other. And for the first time, some of them began to feel lonely. The confusion and dissension left them worse off than they were before. There had to be an answer. It was intolerable without one.

Then, mercifully, someone or something plopped down a picture in their midst. They all stopped what they were saying and doing to look at it.

"It's us!" they shouted without the slightest doubt or hesitation. "At last! Now we know how we fit and where we fit."

In the end, the puzzle was solved and the picture was complete and they all lived happily ever after.

~ 6 ~

Clothes: Who Am I?

W HEN I WAS BORN I came into this world naked and unencumbered. I never gave it much thought. I mean about being naked. The way I looked at it, it didn't really matter. I figured that if I needed clothes I would have been born with them. Or, at the very least, I would have been covered with hair, like dogs and cats.

But that's not what my parents thought. They immediately put strange clothes called diapers on me. Then they got impatient or angry when I soiled them. Was that my fault? I didn't put those clothes on me. I tried to tell them that and that we'd all be better off if I were naked, but it did no good. So I cried instead.

Next they dressed me in blue. That was because I'm a boy. Girls had to wear pink. I don't know why except I think God said so.

The blue I wore went on top of the first layer of clothes, which they called underwear, and not in place of them. As far as I was concerned it meant that there was just more to cover me. A whole lot more. Then again, maybe wearing blue wasn't such a bad idea after all since by then I was getting so covered up with clothes that I wouldn't have known if I was a boy or a girl. But even if I did know, what difference would it have made?

Anyway, by that time I learned that there was another way of telling boys from girls. Boys wore pants and girls wore dresses. Only it didn't always turn out that way. Sometimes it got switched around and I couldn't tell again. Sometimes girls wore pants and men wore funny looking dresses. I found the same confusion about girls having long hair and boys short hair. So I figured God must not have made all these rules or they wouldn't keep changing. Which only made things worse since I couldn't tell when things would change or why. But this I do know. If we didn't wear all these clothes we could just see who we were right off.

As I got older my aunt told me that I looked good in green so I should wear green a lot. Personally, I like red so I wore red a lot. My father thought I looked better in gray, probably because he's rather conservative. My mother liked blue because it complemented my eyes. So I wore the red and green and gray and blue all at the same time to make everybody happy. I also like horizontal stripes, but my uncle said that they made me appear shorter and fatter. My teacher, on the other hand, preferred vertical stripes, which made me taller and thinner. I also learned to wear solid colors for conservative occasions and plaids for informal occasions. Of course I also had to wear sweaters and jackets and mufflers and coats, not to mention socks, shoes, boots, and rubbers.

Then one day in a mad moment of liberation I decided to take it all off and be me once again. Me, unencumbered and unfettered. The naked and real me. I threw off my coat, hat, scarf, and gloves. It was thrilling. I peeled off my plaid jacket, red sweater, mauve vest, and knit tie. I began shaking with excitement. I removed my oxford cordovans, my paisley socks and monogrammed shirt.

Suddenly, I started to get a little nervous. I shyly removed my undershirt. What if someone should happen by? What if someone were to see me this way? Perhaps I could just simply go without an undershirt the way the macho men on television do.

But bare-chested made me feel a little too exposed. Maybe all I really wanted was to be more macho. So why not just replace the monogrammed shirt with a denim one and the mauve vest with a leather one? Next, I exchanged my cordovans for cowboy boots and my paisley jacket for a fringed rawhide one. I put on a ten-gallon Stetson and a string tie.

Well, if nothing else, I had a completely new look.

Twice more in my life I tried to get down to the bare me to discover who I really am. But I never got past my underwear. I tell myself, "What difference does it make? I know what to expect if I ever get past it."

But the truth is I'm really afraid to look. I mean, what if I've been wrong all these years?

 Growing Up

When you're young
you can't wait until you grow up
so that no one can tell you what to do.
Only you won't grow up
until you learn that never happens.

 Death

The more clothes you put on during the day,
the more clothes you have to take off at night.

Tight Little Boxes

WHEN TINY TIM WAS BORN he didn't know and nobody told him that he had just come out of a tight little box. He was free and that felt pretty good because now he could move and stretch without restraint as much as he wanted. He did not miss his box except occasionally and then he would cry.

It wasn't until later that he discovered that everyone around him lived in tight little boxes with just their heads, arms, and feet sticking out. His father had his little box. His mother had her little box. So did his brothers and sisters. Everyone was in tight, neat little boxes.

Was he ever glad he had a box of his own by the time he entered school. All the other children had boxes of their own, and he certainly didn't want to lack anything that everyone else had. Besides, it gave him a sense of security in this new and threatening environment.

It wasn't long before he learned that everything and not just people come in tight little boxes. Lessons come in boxes. Words come in boxes. Even ideas come in their own little boxes.

When he became an adolescent he grew tired of his own tight little box. He wanted to be free to stretch, to move, to dream. But it was frightening to be without the security of his box, so instead he moved from one box to another and another and called that freedom.

Adulthood was no different, even though he thought it might be. In fact, there were just more boxes for him to deal with. There were tight little boxes everywhere — at work, at play, at worship. Everything neat in its own little box making way for other tight little boxes. There was almost no time anymore to dream, and when he did the dreams came in their own boxes.

When he grew old his box seemed to be growing smaller, harder, and tighter. Now there was no room to stretch. The box bent his back and made his bones ache. He wanted to dream, but by now he had forgotten how.

In the end he died. And they buried him — in a tight little box.

 ### The Time to Die

There is never a good time to die.
There are only worse times.

 ### Yes

There is no such thing as a simple "yes."
Every yes has a million little yeses inside it.
"No" is simple.
It has nothing inside it except death.

~ 8 ~

Charlie Atlas
and the Dresser Mirror

W HEN CHARLIE ATLAS was a young teenager, his parents bought him a dresser mirror for his bedroom. Before this whenever he wanted to see what he looked like he used the bathroom mirror to see his face and the full-length mirror in his parent's room to see how he looked when he got all dressed up. Now he had his very own dresser mirror.

One day after he took off his shirt Charlie took a good, long look at himself in the mirror. He was not too pleased with what he saw. His upper torso was not much to look at. His chest was rather scrawny and his biceps were so skinny that he could almost encircle each of them with one hand.

"They're hardly bigger than my wrists," he said as he posed a he-man stance in front of the mirror. "I've got to do something about this or I'll grow up to be puny weakling."

So Charlie began a daily regimen of upper torso exercises. For hours each day and every day he did sit-ups, and pull-ups, and push-ups. He lifted weights, pumped bar bells and dumb bells, stretched springs, and squeezed grips. Slowly but surely his chest grew and his biceps began to bulge. When he saw the progress he was making, he was so pleased that he doubled his efforts. He even went so far as to eat special foods and concentrate on specific exercises. And he did all this with a passion.

The great day finally came when he stood before the dresser mirror and was thrilled beyond words with what he saw. His chest had grown massive with taut and powerful muscles. The biceps on both his arms had ballooned to the point that one would need two hands to span them. His stomach rippled like waves on the seashore. He stood there delighted and enthralled by his image in the mirror.

And then quite unexpectedly, he collapsed. It was not because of overexertion, the doctor told his parents. It was his legs and ankles. They were too weak to hold up the rest of him. In the dresser mirror Charlie could see only his upper body, so that was all he developed.

~ Moral ~

Body mirrors like dresser mirrors only show half of you.
People also need spirit mirrors.

~ 9 ~

The Haunted Castle

HIGH ATOP A HILL overlooking a lush and verdant valley stood a magnificent castle. It had a commanding view of the entire countryside for miles and miles. And for miles and miles it towered in plain view for all people everywhere to see. But no one came near it. No one dared, for it was haunted.

Time and again brave souls ventured forth willing to take up residence in the hapless place, but before long they were driven out by the terrible and unceasing moaning that emanated from every room, hall, nook, and cranny within its stone-cold walls. The longer anyone stayed the louder the groans became until the dirge was so unbearable that they inevitably fled, if not for their lives then for some peace and quiet. In time no one came anymore. Finally, it was decided to level it to the ground and salt its ashes.

Before that day, that awful day of judgment, was to take place, a retired old vicar decided that he would give the sorry castle one last try. Armed with neither bell, book, or candle but only a gentle resolve to save what should not be wasted, he moved in on All Hallows' Eve.

The castle was in a terrible state of disrepair. Heavy layers of dust covered every room the way dirt covers all the graves in a graveyard. Precious little light filtered in and the air was so heavy with death that the old priest could barely breathe. The sun had no sooner gone down when the moaning began.

It was a deep, low, and painful wail that seemed to emerge from the very bowels of the building. It traveled slowly and continually down the dismal corridors and into the endless rooms of the giant castle. Ooooohhhh. Oooooooohhh.

The vicar was not afraid. He had become all too familiar with the sound after long years of pastoring. It no longer evoked terror but sympathy. He walked down the corridors opening doors and listening as if asking the suffering building, "Where does it hurt?" The moaning in the nursery seemed very loud indeed.

He stood there listening intently, trying to pay careful attention to the sound behind the sound. Patiently he waited and eventually he heard it. Behind the moaning he could hear the laughter of children. Then the more the children laughed the more the castle wailed.

"You are crying for the children," the old vicar sighed.

"I am crying for myself," the old castle moaned.

"Why?"

"Because there are no more children in my nursery." Again, the old vicar asked, "Why?" Old folks like young children need fewer words to express themselves.

"Because I frightened them away."

The vicar said nothing. The next question was much too obvious to ask, so the castle answered.

"I was so proud of my freshly painted walls and gaily decorated nursery that it upset me terribly to see the children making a mess of it. Why I was no sooner cleaned when they would again smudge my walls with their grimy little hands and stain my carpets with their silly playthings. The more children there were the greater was my distress until I could bear it no longer."

"So you began to grumble," the old vicar sighed.

"Yes, I did. And with good reason. This was no way to treat a house and they had better start learning it, I said. So I began to grumble."

"And the children were frightened away."

"They went outside to play as they should. They could return later when they learned to behave better."

"Did they?"

"Did they learn to behave better?"

"Did they return?"

"Noooooooooohhhhhh," the castle wailed. "They didn't come back and I didn't want that either. After that the nursery door was closed and now I moan the loss. Ooooooooohhh."

When the vicar walked out of the room, he left the door open behind him. He entered the ballroom next. Here he expected to find gaiety and laughter, but instead he found the same, awful groan. Once again he listened for the sound behind the sound until eventually he heard the lively strains of music. Instruments were playing a spritely tune and heels and shoes were stepping and stamping to the rhythm across the ballroom floor.

"Ooooooohhhh!" the castle wailed.

"It was the feet scuffing the floor, wasn't it?" the old vicar said like a doctor diagnosing a problem.

"My bright, new pretty hardwood floor. Why it was so highly polished that one didn't need a mirror once you entered the room. You just had to look down to see how beautiful everything was. Beautifully decorated walls and magnificently dressed people. I could see it all from above and it was wonderful."

"What do you see now?"

"Dust. Layers and layers of dust. Ooooooooohhhh."

The vicar waited for the moaning to cease. The castle continued. "It was only a slight moaning at first but it annoyed the musicians who had to play louder so as not to hear it. The louder they played the more frantically the dancers danced and the more they scuffed my beautiful floor. Eventually I wailed so loudly that I sent everyone scurrying."

"Now there's no one left," the vicar sighed.

"Nooooooooohh," the castle moaned. "They closed the ballroom door behind them and never came back."

The vicar himself wept as he exited the room. Once again he left the door open behind him. The path he was treading was all too familiar to him. Room after room, door after door the story was the same. The kitchen was too marred, the den too heavy with books, the parlor too cluttered. Some rooms were deemed acceptable, but they could not block out the groans that permeated the entire house. In time all the doors were closed. In the end the front door was closed and the castle was left alone to bemoan its fate.

The old vicar stood at the front door. "Now they will raze you to the ground," he sighed, his voice overcome with sadness.

"Ooooooooooohh. Ooooooooooooooooohh," the castle wailed more pathetically than ever. "Is this the price I must pay for my foolish pride?"

"It is," the vicar cried. "It is the price we must all pay, my friend."

"Then I shall cry until my last stone is leveled to the ground. There is no hoooooope for me. Ooooooooooooohh."

Hope! The mention of the word brought a spark to the old vicar's eye. Hope. That was precisely what he and the castle had both lacked. Overwhelmed with their own grief, they had forgotten how to hope. Their moans had drowned it out. But there was still time. The sun was beginning to rise on the horizon. The townspeople were gathering with their picks and axes and shovels.

"There is hope, my friend. There is always hope," the vicar cried out. "As much for you as there is for me."

"What can we do?" the castle cried. "From my tower I can see the people coming. It is too late."

"It is never too late. That much I have learned from life."

Still the castle would not be consoled. "The moment they come near and hear my moaning, they will tear me down. That is for sure."

"Then stop moaning!" the vicar admonished.

"I can't. Even if I wanted to, I can't. The hurt is too deep and too permanent for me to stop now. What can I do?"

"I don't know," the vicar sighed.

"Then close the front door and leave me to my grief," the castle moaned. "Oooooooooooohhhhhh!"

In the brief silence that followed, the castle's last words echoed in the vicar's mind. Close the door. All the doors in the castle were indeed closed and that was precisely its problem. They had shut life out. It needed to be readmitted.

"Wait! That's it!" the vicar shouted. "We mustn't shut the doors; we must open them."

"What good will that do?" the castle asked.

"We must invite the people in. All the people."

"Then they will hear my crying and run away as they've done so many times in the past."

"No. We must make a new sound over the old sound. We must make the sounds of the living drown out the sounds of the dead. It is the only way. It is the only hope we have."

"It won't work." Even though the castle said it, there was a tinge of nervous hope in its voice. "They will remember the old groans and tear me down."

Remember? Of course, they will remember the vicar thought. That is all they've heard for years. They had grown weary of the incessant groaning and decided to end it. Still, he felt certain that the solution to the problem lay hidden in that very fact. "They will remember," the vicar repeated again and again.

Then it came to him. Of course. How could it be otherwise? Once again life was teaching him that in the very mystery itself lies its own solution and once again the castle had unwittingly opened the door that would eventually save it.

"The children!" the vicar shouted. "Of course, the children."

"Of course the children? What are you ranting about?" the castle asked.

"The children won't remember because they have no memories yet. They will come in. Trust me, my friend. They are our hope. They will come in."

When the villagers arrived at the front door of the castle, they were met by the old vicar.

"Stand aside old man," they shouted. "We have come to destroy this haunted castle."

"Haunted castle, nonsense!" the vicar shouted above their cries.

At that moment the castle could not control itself and groaned a mighty wail. "Ooooooooohhhhh!"

The crowd became dead quiet. "You see," they shouted. "It is haunted."

"Stuff and nonsense," the vicar said. Then very carefully and deliberately he began scanning the crowd as if looking for something or someone. He stopped and called to the old miller's wife. "Martha Higgins, have I not heard you wail a mighty wail on many a sleepless night?"

"You and the whole village too, vicar," Jacob the cobbler added as the townspeople all laughed in agreement.

"It's my arthritis," Martha Higgins objected. "And what about the way you moan over your rheumatism Jacob Mueller?" she shot back, not being one to miss getting in the last word.

"And you, Joseph Peabody," the old vicar continued, knowing his flock that well. "Do you not complain and groan about the bone chilling cold every winter? And you, Sarah Hawkins," he shouted, pointing to the startled woman. "How many times have you wailed over the chores of raising a large family?"

"And it's plenty reason I have too, vicar!" she exclaimed, looking over her brood of ten children.

"Is it all right for us to weep and moan, but not this castle, which has itself fallen on hard times?"

"A castle ain't people, vicar," Tom the blacksmith shouted. "And I for one stand ready to knock the haunted thing down."

"Would a brave and strong man like the village smithy be afraid of what doesn't frighten little children?" the vicar challenged.

Before the blacksmith could bluster a reply, the vicar called to the children. "Children! You have my permission to use the castle for your very own playground. Now go to it."

In a bound Sarah Hawkins's ten children burst through the front door. Without the slightest hesitation all the other children followed. In no time at all, the screaming and shouting of happy, playing children drowned out the castle's sad moans.

The townspeople entered the grand foyer with the vicar. The children were scattered everywhere. They were sliding down the bannisters, swinging from the chandeliers, and sliding across the still highly polished floors that lay hidden beneath years of layered dust.

"The sounds of the living are always enough to overcome the groans of the dead," the vicar said, but no one heard him in all the noise.

But they did hear Sarah Hawkins scream. "Jeremy Hawkins! You stop sliding through all that dust. You're getting yourself as dirty as this old castle."

The vicar laughed. The townspeople laughed. And the old castle laughed for the first time in a long, long time.

~ Moral ~

Houses aren't haunted — people are.
If we close the doors to the rooms of our lives,
then only the dead can inhabit them.

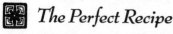 ## The Perfect Recipe

There's no perfect recipe. God is too elusive.

~ 10 ~

Body Language

O NE DAY when the heart was feeling in an especially critical mood, it said to the lungs, "Stop nudging me aside. Who do you think you are anyway? You're so filled with your own self-importance that you're trying to take over the whole place."

"You should talk!" the lungs exploded. "Do you ever march to a different drummer? No! All you do all day long is beat your own drum. The noise is driving me crazy. Come to think of it, I'm sick of it and I'm sick of you."

Well the battle lines were drawn. The two of them continued on this way for days, the one beating the same issue to death while the other just kept blowing hot air about it.

"We'll see about this," the heart finally said, pounding furiously as it told its story to the mouth. The mouth agreed with the heart and bit its lip in anger. "We'll see how swelled up the lungs will be if I hold back," it spat out.

In retaliation the lungs told its story to the stomach. The stomach became very upset and agreed not to feed into the heart's monotonous monologue.

Before long all the other organs began taking sides — the nose with the mouth and lungs, the liver and spleen with the stomach, while the kidneys were split in two.

Alas, the argument never came to a head. Not that it would have done much good, for by this time the body was so divided and weak, it died.

~ Moral ~

Dissension leads to death.

 ### Tyrants

A tyrant who goes unprotested is abetted.

 ### Righteousness

There is very little distance
between being righteous and self-righteous,
and just a short dash gets you there.

~ 11 ~

Cages

ONE DAY A YOUNG LION CUB, feeling the first stirrings of adolescence, wandered away from the pride in order to explore the world. He traveled far, yet not very far, when he came upon the iron bars of a cage. He had never seen anything like them before and was quite confounded by them. He tried to squeeze through but was unable to. He stretched a paw as far as he could to the other side as if that could force him beyond, but it was to no avail. Biting through the bars was hopeless. So in frustration and anguish he paced along the perimeter, searching frantically for some way out.

There was none. Each day he returned to the thick iron bars and restlessly paced back and forth as if pondering his dilemma. There was only one way out. Over the top. But he was too young yet to make the attempt. He was confident that when he was older like the adults of the pride he would have enough height and strength to vault the obstacle. The fact that those who could didn't never occurred to him. He waited impatiently for his day to leap to freedom.

He knew instinctively when the time had come. Over the months he had worn a path along the perimeter of the cage, searching for just the right place. Now he came bounding to it and with a mighty leap hurtled over the top. At last he was free. He celebrated by wildly kicking his hind legs up in the air, chasing his tail, and romping through the high grass. It was wonderful to be free, to be out of the cage that confined the others, never again to face the monotonous pacing of the perimeter. With the bars of the cage at his back he surveyed his new realm. He could see far into the distance and there were no bars. His heart raced with excitement. Now that he was outside he wished to enjoy this new-found freedom. He scampered about running and shouting, "I'm free! I'm free!"

Still, the mere sight of the bars disconcerted him. It would be best to get as far away from this reminder of his confinement as he could. So he bound across the field, putting the bars of the cage far behind him.

But in no time at all he ran into more bars. These were even stronger and higher than the ones he had left behind. He was dumbfounded at first and then angry. Once again he began pacing furiously. There was no going over these. Nor through them. He made several attempts but they ended in frustration. Realizing that he had only jumped from one cage into another enraged him all the more.

He felt more confined than before. For a while he consoled himself by recalling the joy of his escape and the anticipation of exploring his new habitat. But this was short-lived. He was trapped again, and there was no getting away from it.

He examined this new cage carefully and found a place where the bars were not quite as high as elsewhere. He would make his escape there. So, once again with a mighty effort, greater than even he imagined he was capable of, he leaped over the bars.

Once again he somersaulted into the air in jubilation. Only this time he was not about to give full and total reign to his enthusiasm until he made absolutely sure that he really was free.

Unfortunately, he wasn't. Joy was fast becoming a fleeting fancy. He had jumped into still another cage. He immediately raced along its entire circumference with only one objective. While there was still strength in him, he must get free or die.

A final, desperate Herculean effort sent him over the bars once more. This time there was no elation, no wild dance of joy. Only cat-like reserve. Cautiously he moved inward and away from the bars. He traveled far, but still not far enough to satisfy him. Certainly not far enough to start celebrating.

When he had gone a considerable distance he noticed an old lion seated in the high grass. He approached him cautiously. Then he recognized him. It was the father of his pride.

"I see you've returned," the old lion said, moving his eyes toward him but not his head.

"How can you sit there so peacefully?" the young lion roared. "Don't you know you're in a cage?"

"I know," the old lion said. "I know. But, from where I sit, there are no bars."

~ Moral ~

True freedom always lies within.

 Character

The real test of character is not how you do in victory but how you deal with defeat.

~ 12 ~

The Lady of the Lake

WHEN SHE WAS A LITTLE GIRL her parents bought a cottage by the lake. It was a tiny thing like so many others around it, humble but soon to be rich in memories. They went swimming almost every day during the summer and on special occasions her father would rent a row boat and they would paddle all around the lake. During those wonder years she learned how to fish and swim. She even once tried water-skiing. Vacations were a constant joy because of that little cottage by the lake.

As she grew older she found other interests. Clothes, parties, friends, and especially boys began to occupy most of her time. She had even taken to going to summer school to further her education and social life. The few times she went to the cottage were a still a delight because now she went with her friends. Horseplay in the water, long walks along the beach, and toasting marshmallows at night added more luster to her enjoyment of the place.

After she married she was much too busy to go there very often, if at all. Even when her parents died and left her the cottage, she could not summon up the resolve or the energy to make much use of it. Besides, it didn't suit her taste anymore. The cottage was small and inconvenient. It would need extensive remodeling in order to satisfy all her needs. Even the lake itself now seemed to be nothing more than an oversized pond. If only it were bigger. If only the cottage were a bit more. She considered selling it but thought that her children might enjoy it. However, whenever they went there her attitude rubbed off on them, so they rarely enjoyed it. In the end, she just abandoned it.

After the kids were married, she gave the lake a few more tries, but it was no longer a part of her life. There were just too many other important things to do. She was an accomplished and successful woman. She was lecturing and traveling a great deal, still working hard to maintain a palatial home in the suburbs.

She was on one of her business trips when her secretary called her about the news. Some vandals had broken into the cottage and set it afire. It had burned to the ground. It didn't really matter, but some strange compulsion brought her back there. It had been a long time. She stood amid the charred rubble and remembered. Unaccountably, tears began to fill her eyes. Then she knew. Suddenly, she knew that if her mansion, her car, her clothes, and all that she had had gone up in smoke, she would not have cried as hard as she did for that tiny little cottage on that small lake.

By the time she left, the lake seemed bigger once again. Her tears had made it so.

~ Moral ~

Nothing that enriches our lives is insignificant.

Little Johnny Sunshine:
A Tale of the Christ

ONCE UPON A TIME there was a gray and dismal place called the Land of Gloom. The sun never shone there because the sky from one end to the other was always full of thick, heavy clouds that never allowed any of the sun's rays to shine through. The days were long and dreary and the nights were black as pitch.

The poor people of Gloom never laughed or smiled or even knew what those things meant since they never had sunshine to brighten their days or their spirits. There was no joy in the Land of Gloom.

On one dull day as unmemorable as all the other dreary days a boy named Johnny went out into the woods to gather broken branches. It was a chore he especially didn't like because the forest with its thick canopy of leaves was even darker and gloomier than the village. This day Johnny had to penetrate deeper into the forest than he cared to since all the fallen branches at the edge of the woods had already been hastily gathered by the other children of the village. They were all afraid of going too far into the Dark Forest.

Johnny thought of nothing else but gathering his stack of wood as quickly as possible and hurrying back home. As he rushed from tree to tree picking up fallen branches, the wind picked up and began to blow harder and fiercer. There was no way of telling if this was a storm wind or not since in the Land of Gloom the sky was always gray. But in the deep dark of the forest it seemed even more frightening than usual. In no time at all the wind became violent, forcing even the biggest of trees to bend before it. The thick covering above him was being torn apart so violently that the scattering leaves seemed to be racing him out of the forest. Johnny dropped his bundle and began to run.

Then, quite suddenly, he stopped frozen in his tracks. Just above him, the wind tore a hole in the forest ceiling. Through this unusual window Johnny could see the clouds blowing furiously across the sky. The sight of so many immense clouds moving so quickly and changing shapes so rapidly both fascinated and terrified him.

While he stood there immobilized, it happened. It was something that couldn't happen again in a hundred years, or a hundred thousand years. The wind blew a hole through the clouds. For the first time ever in the Land of Gloom or the Dark Forest, light from the sun burst through. It came streaming down and found its way through the hole in the forest covering. A beam of sunlight shone on the forest floor just in front of Johnny.

He stared in awe at it. He had never seen anything like it in his whole life. Nor had anyone ever told him that there was even such a thing. He was sure that no one in the Land of Gloom had ever seen anything like this or he would have heard about it. Yet, here it was and he couldn't take his eyes off it. Then, without knowing why, he began to feel good all over. A warm glow filled his whole body until it took away the chill of the wind and his fear. It was a wonderful feeling like nothing he had ever known in his whole life. While he stared at it, enjoying this strange, new sensation, he suddenly began to smile. It just came upon him automatically. He didn't think it or will it. He couldn't have even if he wanted to since he had never seen a smile or knew what it was. But there it was on his face. A grin from ear to ear.

He could have stayed there forever, just staring at that wonderful ray of sunlight and feeling good all over. But the wind was still blowing, and he was afraid that it would blow it away and he would never see that wonderful sight again or ever again know that marvelous feeling. He must capture it before it could get away. He quickly reached to his belt, where he carried a sack. His fingers fumbled nervously with the drawstrings as he ran to the spot. Quick as a flash he covered the spot of sunlight with his sack and closed it up tight.

At that moment, the forest became gloomy once again. But Johnny didn't care. He had captured his prize and raced all the way home with it. He ran past his mother and father without answering their questions and closed himself up in his small upstairs room. He lit the lamp on his bed stand and sneered at its poor glow. He had something now that shone a thousand times more brightly; and it was his, all his.

~

He lay on his bed remembering that wonderful sight and the marvelous feeling it gave him. Now it was his to have again and again whenever he wanted it. All he would have to do is open his sack and it would be there waiting for him.

But what if he hadn't captured it? What if it had somehow gotten out? Then all he would have was a memory. And who would believe him?

He sat up and looked at the sack lying on his stool. He reached for it carefully. When he took it in his hands the cloth felt warm and comfortable.

"You're in there!" he shouted. "I did get you."

"Yes, I am," said a voice from within the sack.

This so shocked Johnny that he dropped the bundle to the floor. The strings of the sack loosened and suddenly the room was filled with a blinding light. Johnny looked around him with amazement. Not all the lamps in the house could have made his room this bright. Once again, that warm, good feeling came over him. He wasn't afraid anymore.

"It's wonderful," he cried.

The voice from the sack spoke again. "Why have you brought me here?"

"Who are you?" Johnny stammered a little nervously.

"I'm a sunbeam."

"What's that?" Now it was the sunbeam's turn to be perplexed. "What do you mean? Do you mean that you don't know what a sunbeam is?"

"I don't know. What is it?"

"Why, I'm a beam of sunlight."

"What's sunlight?" Johnny asked. Talking was beginning to take away the awkwardness of the situation.

"You don't know what sunlight is? Sunlight is what you see by."

"I see with my eyes," Johnny said.

"Of course," said the sunbeam. "But you can't see in the dark, can you?"

"No one can see in the dark," he answered. "You've got to have light to see by."

"And where does that light come from?"

"From the lamp." Then he thought for a moment. "And from the fire."

"Where does daylight come from?" the sunbeam asked patiently.

"From the day!" Johnny answered triumphantly.

For a moment, the sunbeam didn't know what to say. Rather than continue with the questions and answers he decided to just tell him. "Daylight comes from the sun."

"What's the sun?" Johnny asked.

The sunbeam realized that he was going to have to be very patient with this boy and explain things carefully. "The sun is a great big ball of fire in the sky"

"There is no great big ball of fire in the sky. There's only clouds."

"You mean you have never seen the sun?" the sunbeam asked unbelievingly.

"How can I see what isn't there?"

"Of course it's there. Where do you think I came from?"

"I don't know. I've never seen anything like you."

"Well, there is a sun, and that's where I'm from. The sun is high up in the sky above the clouds. It shines down on you every day even if you don't know it. That's what gives you the daylight that you see by."

Johnny thought about this in silence for a while but decided that he couldn't really understand it. "How could it be there if I can't see it?" he asked.

"Because of the clouds."

"Then how do I know it's there?"

"You see me, don't you?"

"Yes."

"Then if you see me, you see the sun. That's where I come from."

Again, Johnny pondered this for a while. "Well, I've certainly never seen anything like you before. I don't think anyone else has either, or I would have heard about it."

"Well, now that you've got me what do you intend to do with me?" the sunbeam asked.

"I really don't know. I'm going to have to think about it."

However, this was about all that Johnny felt he could handle for one day, so he said goodnight to his sunbeam and tied up the sack once again. He placed it on the stool next to his bed and lay down to go to sleep.

Sleep did not come easily. It had been a most strange and peculiar day. There was so much to think about. Was there really a sun? There had to be, or where did this strange creature come from? Could this sunbeam be bad? That wasn't likely. Everything about it made him feel warm and good. Just knowing that it was beside his bed made him feel strangely comfortable and secure. What was he going to do with it tomorrow? He didn't know, but he was too tired to think anymore about it. He fell soundly asleep.

~

When he awoke the next morning he thought that whole affair was nothing more than a dream. He dressed and went off to school, never even thinking of the sack that still lay on his bedside stool.

After he had finished his chores and sat by the evening fire warming himself, he remembered his strange dream. His father sat next to him, working on a harness by the dim light of the fire.

"Father, what is the sun?"

"Why do you ask, my boy?" He stopped what he was doing and gave the boy a puzzled look.

Johnny was reluctant to tell him about his strange dream. Dreams were nonsense and never to be taken seriously. He couldn't think of how to answer his father.

When he didn't answer his father chided him. "You shouldn't be listening to old wives' tales. They'll just fill your head with stuff and nonsense."

Later, when Johnny asked his mother, she said, "I'm sure I don't know."

Johnny sat there pondering these remarks when it suddenly occurred to him. How could he have dreamt it if he had never heard of such a thing? Was it really true? Did it actually happen?

He raced upstairs to his room. The sack still lay on the stool. He reached for it. It was warm.

His heart leapt within him. He fumbled with the drawstrings and opened it. Light burst forth and filled the room. Johnny had to rub his eyes until he could see again.

"It's true! It wasn't a dream," he shouted.

"Why did you doubt me?" the sunbeam asked.

"My father said that it's just a foolish tale and my mother never heard of the sun."

"Well, now that you've seen me again, do you believe?"

"Yes, I do."

"What do you intend to do with me?" the sunbeam asked.

"I'm going to take you downstairs and show you to my father and mother."

"Are you sure you want to do that?"

The question took him by surprise. Why wouldn't he do that? Johnny thought about it. This light gave him a wonderful, warm feeling unlike any he had ever experienced before. What if he brought it to his parents and they took it away from him? He might never see it again, might never feel that feeling again. What if they were afraid of it and threw the sack outside? He would lose it forever. It would vanish out there like a flash of lightning. Maybe that's what I caught, he thought. A flash of lightning. Maybe there is no sun after all.

True or not, lightning or not, he decided to keep it to himself and for himself. He would take it out whenever he had a mind to and if he had a mind to. He caught it and it belonged to him. He tired quickly of all this heavy thinking. He just wanted to enjoy it. So he smiled and twirled round and round in his light-drenched room, never imagining that one day this would be called dancing. When he was finished, he closed up the bag and went to bed.

~

Secrets are hard to keep. Especially for children. Johnny just had to tell someone. His closest friend was the neighboring farmer's daughter, Maria. He decided to share his secret treasure with her. He took her upstairs to his room and made her promise that she wouldn't tell a soul what he was going to show her.

"If I tell you a secret, do you promise not to tell anyone?"

"I promise."

"Solemn promise?"

"Solemn promise."

"Cross your heart and hope to die?"

"Cross my heart and hope to die."

When he untied the strings the room once again became flooded with light.

Maria immediately covered her eyes. Johnny laughed.

"What is it, Johnny?" she asked, keeping her eyes covered.

Afraid that she might think it was lightning and run out of the house before he could stop her, Johnny quickly said, "It's a sunbeam, you don't have to be afraid. Look."

Slowly Maria took her hands away from her eyes. The sight of the room bathed in light brought a smile to her face. "It's wonderful," she cried.

Johnny began twirling around, his arms outstretched, laughing all the while. The same wonderful feeling took hold of Maria too, and she followed suit. They spun themselves around almost to dizziness. When they sat down to rest Maria asked him where he got this amazing light. Johnny told her the story of his adventure in the Dark Forest.

"But how do you know where it comes from?" she asked.

"The sunbeam told me," he said.

"You mean it talks?" she asked, suddenly frightened.

Seeing her fear, he assured her, "You don't have to be afraid. It's very friendly."

Johnny walked over to the sack and said, "I've brought you a friend."

"I know Maria," it said.

"How do you know me?" she asked.

"Why, I've seen you many times," the sunbeam replied.

"But I've never seen you. Never."

"Of course, you have. Everyday you've seen me. I'm sunlight."

"What's sunlight?"

"I'm light from the sun. I'm what you call daylight," it said, remembering the conversation with Johnny.

Johnny quickly told her about the sun.

"That's amazing," Maria said. "Well, I'd like to thank you Mr.

Sunbeam for making me feel so wonderful. I never felt this way before."

"You're welcome, I'm sure," the sunbeam replied.

"May I come to see you again?"

"So long as I'm still around you're welcome to."

This reply startled Johnny. "What do you mean so long as you're still around? I don't want you to ever leave. I won't ever let you go."

"I'm afraid that's not entirely up to you. You see, I can't stay away from the sun too long. I get my power from the sun. If I don't go back I will lose all my power and die. I'm already getting weaker."

He didn't seem any weaker to Johnny. His light was still blinding. "I'm sure you'll last a long time," Johnny said hopefully.

"Not as long as you may think or want," he replied.

"I would certainly hate to lose you, now that I've met you," Maria said innocently. "Is there anything we can do?"

"We'll see," the sunbeam replied.

～

The next day was not quite as happy for Johnny. The thought of losing this wonderful friend — yes, that's what he was beginning to think of the sunbeam as, his friend — was almost too much to bear. Maria wasn't any help either. She wanted to show him to others before he left so they too could enjoy him. Johnny stubbornly refused. Opening up the sack too much might weaken him all the faster. The answer was not to overdo it. But she argued that being away from the sun was what weakened him, and therefore they should take care not to waste time.

"Wouldn't it be better for others to see and enjoy what we have experienced?"

Johnny had to agree with her logic. However, they would only show it to a few close friends at first. So, little by little their friends came over to the house and experienced the great wonder. Of course, it soon ceased being a secret. Even if the children hadn't told a soul, the smiles on their faces, the happiness in their attitudes betrayed the presence of something unusual in their lives. The word was spreading. More and more people were coming to see the great wonder.

Then there were those who couldn't come to Johnny's house, like the old and the sick. They too had heard of this marvelous thing and did not want to be left out. Johnny readily agreed to bring his sack to them. But he must never open it outside. If he ever opened the sack outside, he was afraid that they would immediately lose the sunbeam altogether, for now he could see that the light was not as bright as it first was.

~

Slowly but surely the Land of Gloom was changing. Something new and different and wonderful was happening. People were beginning to smile and even laugh. Joy was becoming common in more and more places. Johnny had no idea how much longer all this would last, but he was happier now than he had ever been. He and the sunbeam had become fast friends. The only thing that saddened him was seeing the sunbeam's power growing weaker. But he had no regrets. Maria had been right.

But all was not well in the land. All the attention the sunbeam was getting was causing a stir among a number of people. There were complaints about children lacking in seriousness, even about adults becoming frivolous. Certain elders were especially upset over the new practice of merrymaking and dancing. The cause of the problem was this strange and mysterious sack. They said that it could only be evil and therefore must be destroyed before it could do more harm.

The town council met in secret. They argued about how they could manage to get hold of the evil sack. Stealing it might turn many of the people against them. To take it forcibly from the boy would have the same effect. They debated well into the night before they came up with a solution. The next day they sent for Maria.

"Tell us, child, about this strange sack."

"There's nothing strange about it," she answered innocently.

"But we hear that it perform all kinds of magic tricks. It makes blind people see and deaf people hear and sick people feel well again. Is that not strange?"

"Oh, it's the sunbeam that does that. Not the sack," she replied.

"Sunbeam, child? What's a sunbeam?"

"It's light from the sun."

"There is no such thing! It is an old wives' tale. Have you ever seen this so-called sun?"

"No."

"Has anyone else seen it?"

"Not that I know of."

"Then there is none."

"Then where does the bright light in the sack come from?" she challenged more than asked.

The inquisitor was about to erupt angrily over her impertinence, but managed to suppress it. He could outsmart this simple child.

"Have you ever seen lightning, my child."

"Yes."

"Have you ever seen what lightning can do?"

"Yes," she replied nervously, losing some of her confidence.

"It can destroy houses, shatter trees, and KILL. Are you aware of that?"

"Yes, sir, but I don't think it's lightning."

"YOU DON'T THINK!" he screamed. "It is our responsibility to think. It is yours to obey your elders. We tell you that through some evil magic this sack contains lightning that will destroy our land."

"But it hasn't done anything like that. It's made people happy."

"Hah! That's precisely the way it works. You are but a child. What can you know of these things? Once it has cast its spell over the people and they are powerless to stop it, it will turn against us and destroy our land, our homes, our families. We must stop it before it's too late."

Maria was weakening, but she continued valiantly.

"Please, sir. I find that hard to believe. It has never done anything but good. How can it be bad if it does good?"

"For how long?" he shouted.

Maria remembered that the sunbeam told them that it was losing its power. What did it mean? Would it do something terrible before it left, like the inquisitor suggested? She was not quite so certain about anything anymore.

The inquisitor caught her hesitation. What he said made the girl hesitate, so he repeated it. "For how long?"

"Not much longer," she replied.

"And why not?" he pushed on.

"Because it's losing its power."

"Precisely!" There was a general murmur among the elders. "If it's getting weak, it may try to destroy us while it still has enough power. There is no time to waste. Don't you see what it's trying to do, child? It's trying to distract us, lull us into thinking it's our friend in order to get us off guard. Then it will strike. Believe me it will strike and strike without warning. I tell you we must act first and fast."

This was too much for the poor girl. She gave in. "What can I do?" she asked.

The inquisitor relaxed. He changed his attitude toward her. He tried to sound warm and understanding. "I know it must be difficult for you to find out that you've been tricked and used. But you may have heard something that can help us to capture this thing and destroy it. Can you think of anything at all?"

Maria thought for a while. "There is something Johnny told me. He said we must never open the sack outside or we will lose it altogether."

"There you have it!" the inquisitor exclaimed. "You see, once it is released outdoors its power is lost. It is our only hope. We must get hold of this sack."

The assembly agreed. A secret plan must be put into action and quickly. They decided to carry it out the following evening.

~

When supper was done and evening chores were finished, Johnny and all his friends gathered in front of the house. There was disturbing news. The town constable and some elders were on their way over. Courageously, Johnny and his friends decided that there was no way that they would allow them to enter the house. Even if they did the sack was well hidden and they would never tell where. They would all stick together come what may.

By the time the constable and the inquisitor reached the house, so many others joined them that they had become an angry mob. They surrounded the house.

The sight of so many shouting people frightened the children. Many of them ran off in terror. Just a few brave souls remained to stand them off.

"Give us the sack!" the constable demanded.

"Never," Johnny cried.

"Behave yourselves and give us what we ask or you will all be punished."

"We haven't done anything wrong," Johnny protested.

"What do you know?" the constable stormed. "You are just foolish children. You are playing with fire, and we're going to stop you before you do any more damage."

"What damage?" Johnny was sobbing uncontrollably now. He was terrified of these angry people and confused by their charges.

"Tell us where the sack is!" the constable shouted impatiently.

The others began screaming, "Where is it?" "Give it to us!" Menacingly, the crowd began closing in on them.

Just then Maria emerged from the back door and ran to the inquisitor, who was waiting for her. She handed the sack over to him. The planned diversion had worked.

When the constable saw this he called to the mob. "No need to go any further. We have what we want."

Johnny wondered what he meant. He turned around and saw Maria and the inquisitor hurrying off together. He yelled to her at the top of his lungs, "Maria! What have you done?"

Things began happening rapidly now, the way they usually do when they're out of control. The crowd was heading back to the town square where the council of elders awaited them. Johnny ran along behind them shouting and protesting, but to no avail.

It seemed that they all converged on the square at the same time — the inquisitor, Maria, the shouting mob, and sobbing Johnny.

"I have the evil thing!" the inquisitor cried, holding the sack up in his hand.

"Destroy it!" the crowd yelled. "Destroy it!"

"Please, no!" Johnny cried, barely able to be heard above the shouts of the crowd. "Please don't."

The council of elders deliberated for less than a minute. "Destroy it!" they ordered. The inquisitor started to untie the drawstrings. He fumbled with them but couldn't undo the knot.

As a last desperate measure, Johnny hurled himself at the inquisitor. "No!" he screamed and knocked him over. The two of them lay sprawled on the ground with the sack just out of reach. The inquisitor stretched out for it but Johnny frantically held him back. The inquisitor struggled to free himself, but Johnny held him off with all his might. The crowd shouted angrily, "Destroy it. Destroy it."

Then, quite suddenly, the inquisitor reached into his pocket, took out a knife, and quick as lightning plunged it into the sack.

There was a blinding flash of light as the bag burst open. In the dark of the night the light was brighter and more brilliant than it had ever been before. The entire crowd fell back in awe and amazement. The brilliance lit up the clouds more brightly than a thousand strokes of lightning. The village and everything in it from the biggest house to the tiniest blade of grass was awash with blinding light. The Dark

Forest gleamed with the light of a thousand years. It was as something that had never happened before and will never happen again.

It lasted only a moment. But that moment seemed like forever. Only Johnny's voice shattered the awful silence. "NO!" he screamed. He cried out with all that was in him, from the very depths of his being until there was no more breath, no more life in him. He had fallen upon the sack a mere moment after it was split open. He made a desperate attempt to save the sunbeam, to keep it from spilling out and dying. But he was too late. His hands reached it a split second too late. He lay on the earth sobbing, the torn sack in his trembling hands.

There was a little faint glimmer of light left in the sack. "I'm sorry," Johnny cried. "I'm sorry," his tears falling into the gaping knife wound. A faint voice emerged from the sack. Had Johnny not been kneeling on the ground so close to it he would not have heard it. "I know," it said.

"I love you," Johnny sobbed as he bent over and kissed the open wound. The light flickered out.

~

Darkness returned to the Land of Gloom. Clouds covered the sky day in and day out the way they always had. The Dark Forest remained as dark and frightening as ever. And, for the most part, the incident of the sack and the sunbeam was put out of mind. The inquisitor and the elders had convinced the villagers that they been saved from a great evil. The sick who had been healed got sick again. The old people began acting their age once more. Everything had returned to normal and dismal.

Everything except Johnny. There was something about him. Something different. No one knew quite what it was but it was there all right. There was a kind of gleam in his eyes, unlike anyone else's.

The inquisitor and the elders said to leave things alone and in time everyone would forget all about what happened. But Maria couldn't forget what she had done. She had to make amends to Johnny. Tear-filled and remorseful she went to him and apologized for her awful betrayal.

"They tricked me," she sobbed. "I didn't know what I was doing."

Johnny tried to console her but she couldn't stop crying. Finally, he said to her, "If I tell you a secret, do you promise not to tell anyone?"

Maria took her hands away from her eyes and looked at him through her tears. "I promise," she said.

"Solemn promise?"

"Solemn promise."

"Cross your heart and hope to die?"

"Cross my heart and hope to die."

"Do you remember when the sack was cut open and the light came out and flashed all over everywhere?"

"I do," she sobbed, "and because of me the sunbeam is gone for good."

"It didn't all go out, Maria. There was still a little left in my sack."

"There was?"

"Yes, there was. Just a little and it was flickering out. So I told it how sorry we were and kissed it good-bye.

"I'm so glad the sunbeam found that out before it died."

"Maria," Johnny whispered secretively. "It didn't die."

"It didn't?" Maria looked at Johnny curiously. "Then what happened to it?"

"When I kissed it," he said, his voice taking on a strange almost mystical quality, "it didn't go out like the rest of the light." He paused remembering the moment. Then, as if in a trance, he said, "What was left came inside me."

Suddenly, Johnny's face lit up like never before. He was radiant. Mary knew now that the wonderful sunbeam didn't die. It was still alive and there for everyone to see. And the people did see it and they didn't forget because from that day on everyone called him Little Johnny Sunshine.

~ 14 ~

The Lonely Little Pine Tree

THE EARLY MORNING OCTOBER sun peeked over the mountain-top, spreading its welcome warmth on the chilled valley below. Little Tree felt it and shook off his light coat of snow into the breeze. He looked down at the valley far below. As the sunlight made its way past the shadow of the mountain it moved across the woods like a forest fire in a blaze of autumn colors.

"Wow! Is that ever beautiful," he said to no one. There was no one to say it to since he was perched way up there all by himself. There was no other tree or shrub anywhere near him on the mountaintop. It was lonely up there by himself, but he had never thought about it before. He was just simply here and everything else was down there. Now as he surveyed the world beneath him as if for the first time, he noticed how all alone he really was.

"There's a clump of trees over there," he said. "And clumps over there and there," he added, looking even more closely. "And whole big bunches of them everywhere. But I'm all alone."

"You are not alone," a voice said. "I am here with you."

Little Tree looked around and saw no one.

"Who said that?" he asked.

"I did," the voice answered.

"Who are you?" Little Tree wondered if the voice was being carried up on a breeze from the valley below. Or was it coming from the sky above? He couldn't tell.

"I am the Tree Spirit," the voice said.

"Where are you?" Little Tree asked.

"I am all around you," the Tree Spirit said, pausing for a moment, "and in you. That's why you can hear me and I can hear you."

"Where did you come from? I've been here for quite some time and I've never seen you..." Little Tree stammered, realizing that he couldn't actually see the Tree Spirit. "I've never heard you before."

"I've always been here. Ever since the first tree made its appearance on earth I have been here. No tree has ever really been alone."

"How come you never spoke to me before?" Little Tree asked.

"Because you didn't need me before," the Tree Spirit said simply.

It was true. Little Tree had been perfectly content before, living and growing on the mountaintop. It wasn't until just now that for the first time in his life he really noticed the others and saw what they had and he didn't. It was the colors that first dazzled him. Why there were trees down there dressed in all kinds of marvelous colors — deep red and bright gold and warm orange — while he was simply green? Always green. Ever green.

The Tree Spirit knew what Little Tree was thinking without his having to speak. "The leaves on those trees are dying because winter is coming. So I make their short life end in a wonderful blaze of glory. Your leaves will live through the winter."

"But my leaves are not nearly as big or as pretty as all the others," he complained, this time out loud so that he could hear himself as well as be heard.

"True," the Tree Spirit said. "But if you were to have big leaves the strong winds up here would blow them off. Without your leaves you could not grow and survive. That's why I made your leaves thin and needle sharp so that they could cut through the wind and remain strong."

"Still, I have no friends and the others do," Little Tree cried, which was the reason for this whole conversation in the first place.

"Look closely at the others," the Tree Spirit said, "and tell me what you see."

"I see trees surrounded by trees and trees and trees. I even see pine trees like me surrounded by other pine trees."

"Look closely now and tell me what else you see," the Spirit said.

Little Tree stared very hard. That's when he noticed that where all the trees were clumped closely together their lower limbs were either weak and scrawny or they were dead. Even the evergreens had lost most of their beautiful green leaves."

"You have to pay the price," the Tree Spirit said. Little Tree looked at the great sprawl of the world before him and heaved a mighty sigh, which the wind carried to the forest below.

"I guess I'm really all right just the way I am," he said.

"I guess you really are," the Tree Spirit answered.

 Nature

Nature is God's other Bible.
Like with the written one,
you have to take time and learn how to read it.

 Why God Made the World Round

God made the world round so that no matter
how small or insignificant you think you are,
wherever you are standing on it
you are at the top of the world.

The Wall and Bernie Schwarz

A YOUNG MAN had a dream, or perhaps a vision. He looked out his bedroom window and saw that next door to his a house a carnival had suddenly sprung up, complete with roller coasters, ferris wheels, merry-go-rounds, and innumerable people enjoying themselves. He immediately hurried out of the house to join the happy throng, when he ran smack up against a high stone wall that separated him from the carnival. When he tried to scale it, he found that there was no place for him to grab hold. Going through the wall was hopeless, for it was impenetrably thick. Nor was he able to go around it, for it stretched endlessly in both directions. There was just no way for him to get beyond the wall. He could only pound his fists against it in frustration and cry.

Then he heard someone calling out to him. The voice came from above. There was someone on top of the wall yelling down to him. He said, "Get others!"

"Why?" he asked.

"It's the only way to get over the wall."

After thinking about it, the young man realized that it was his only hope to make it over the wall. He had to find others who would stand one on top of another until they reached the top. Then they could pull themselves up and over. He judged that it would take only four others to do the trick.

He went in search of helpers and readily found three others. Without a fourth however, they could not reach the top and scale the wall. He needed to find only one more.

He could find only one more. It was Bernie Schwarz. He hated Bernie Schwarz. Ever since he was a kid he hated Bernie Schwarz. It had started with a snowball fight that ended in a fist fight, and they hadn't spoken to each other ever since. Look as he might he couldn't find another person anywhere. There was no making it without a fifth person. It was Bernie Schwarz or nothing.

~ Moral ~

So too heaven.

 Paradise

Why is it that for so much of our life
it seems that paradise is just around the corner
or over the next hill?
Then, all too late, we discover
that we've already turned the corner,
and we've over the hill.

~ 16 ~

The Squirrel and the Pine Tree

ONE DAY a great and mighty pine tree said to a squirrel playing among its branches, "There is a treasure waiting for you at the very tip of my topmost branch."

The tree itself was a treasure, thought the squirrel, who nested in its branches and feasted on pine nuts. But she could not resist the lure of a treasure trove that awaited her at the top.

The climb indeed would be arduous and long, since it was by far the tallest tree in the forest. A plan was needed. She would collect all the nuts on one level, then climb and store them at the next level. This would give her nourishment and strength to work the next level and so on and so on until she reached the summit.

The lower branches were thick, firm, and fruit-laden so the squirrel ate well and moved heavily among the limbs. But the higher she climbed, the thinner and more pliant the limbs became. There were also fewer nuts for the squirrel to eat. However, the squirrel herself became thinner and put less strain on the slighter branches.

As she climbed yet higher, there was even less to eat, and the branches beneath her bowed ever more dangerously. Were she to feast at this height, she would most surely fall to her death. She began to wonder what treasure the top of the tree could hold that was worth all this difficulty and peril. Would it not be better to just go back down?

But the summit was in sight. Now there were no more nuts to be had. The squirrel was dangerously thin and weak. Even with her frail weight, she had to move infinitely slowly and carefully.

She struggled forward until the top was but a short climb away. What would the treasure be? She had never thought to ask the tree. No need to now. She was almost there. She would see for himself.

At last she reached the pinnacle. Holding tightly, the squirrel and the limb swayed precariously in the strong wind.

But there was no treasure here! No pine nut of incredible size or indescribable taste. She had simply climbed to the top. Had the tree tricked her? It was all for naught.

Disappointed and frustrated, she turned around to head back. As she did, she looked out. The entire forest lay spread out before her. She could see for miles and miles in every direction. The view was breathtaking. She held fast there... and would have stayed forever, but the sun was beginning to set.

When at last she descended and told all the other squirrels of her great discovery, it was said among them that she was never hungry again.

 Soul Food

*Food for the soul is always more filling
than food for the body.*

~ 17 ~

The Woodsman and the Dragon

ONE DAY a woodsman and his son were in the forest gathering wood when they came upon a baby dragon. The woodsman would gladly have continued on his way content to leave well enough alone but not his curious and impressionable son. The boy was intrigued by the creature and pleaded passionately for permission to bring it home with them.

"Dragons take a great deal of care," the wary father commented, "and if not treated properly can turn on you."

"I will take good care of him," the boy responded all too quickly.

The boy did as he promised. He fed, sheltered, protected, and provided for all the needs of his wonderful pet. They were inseparable. They ate together, played together, slept together, and grew up together.

When the boy became a young man he said to his father, "I thought when dragons grew up they were supposed to breathe fire. Why doesn't mine?"

"Because yours is contented. Only angry dragons breathe fire," he said.

Not wanting his dragon to lack any of the essentials of dragonhood and curious to make sure that it wasn't any different from all the other dragons, the young man decided to get some fire out of the beast. He took a stick and began to prod the animal. At first the dragon responded playfully. But continual poking began to irritate it. Smoke came snorting out of its nostrils. A solid whack on the head brought a sudden explosion of flame, which set fire to the grass at the young man's feet and scorched him in the process. It had worked, but he realized that he had better be careful. The dragon for its part was not amused.

Such knowledge, however, was of no value unless it could be put to some useful end. The dragon could very well serve a good purpose, for example, by lighting all the evening fires, A few well-placed pokes and the beast ceased being just an adornment or a keepsake. He had become a servant as well as a pet.

The young man grew into an adult. The dragon also grew to full stature. Now there was hardly ever any time for play or companionship. The man was too busy. The dragon was too idle.

One day the man had to clear away some brush. The work was difficult and time-consuming. "Why not put the dragon to work and let him burn it away," he thought.

This task was more demanding than simply lighting the evening fire, and the beast did not take kindly to it. The man had to prod more, poke more before the dragon responded the way it was being urged to.

Each time the man had to clear another field he noticed it was taking less and less to provoke the beast. He was pleased at how quickly the giant was learning and how readily it was responding. After thinking about it, he was sure that there were countless other ways that the dragon could be used. He must try them. All of them.

The next day he led the dragon into the woods to try out some new ideas. He prodded the beast, but it stubbornly would not respond. Again and again he tried. The dragon simply stood there sullenly snorting smoke. The man then took a heavy stick and gave it a good, hefty whack on the nose. The dragon responded. The man was incinerated.

The beast lumbered back into the forest it had come from.

~ Moral ~

One can provoke order just so much.

 ### The Fox and the Hare

A fox and a hare went off hunting together.
The fox returned alone.

 ### Wisdom

Experience comes with age.
Wisdom profits from the experience.

 ### The Flea and the Ant

"I have taught man to be industrious,"
said the ant to the flea.
"And I have taught him to be grateful," said the flea.

~ 18 ~

Joseph's Ark

DURING THE DAYS when God appointed Judges to rule over the tribes of Israel, the Ark of the Covenant was lost for a brief period. Without the touchstone of their devotion to Yahweh, the people were falling away from true worship. The Ark was the focal point of their worship, their gathering place for prayer. It was the throne of God. Without it they had simply begun to drift away, the way a twig breaks away from the pull of a whirlpool. Unless the Ark were recovered or a new Ark were to take its place, the high priest feared that there would eventually be no faith left in Israel.

Thus, he commissioned that every artisan throughout Israel craft a new Ark, one that would be a fitting and appropriate replacement for the old one. Then God Himself could choose its worthy successor.

As it was decreed, so it happened. Every craftsman without exception set about the task of building a truly noble and worthwhile replacement for the Ark. From the greatest to the least all the artisans applied theirs talents to the best of their ability with the finest materials at their disposal. In the end there were almost numberless Arks to choose from.

When the day of decision finally arrived there lay spread before the people of Israel some of the greatest works anyone had ever seen. There were chests of wood and stone and bronze and silver and gold. Some boasted inlaid ivory, others ornately carved figures. Still others dazzled with precious gems. God Himself would have difficulty choosing from among so many inspiring and marvelous offerings.

Before each ark the high priest cast his sacred die to determine the Lord's choice. One by one the offerings were rejected. Then the high priest arrived at Joseph's ark. Joseph was a poor carpenter with only normal ability but deep devotion to God. His ark was painfully simple and decidedly lackluster. When the die turned up positive the people were outspokenly upset.

"What can this mean?" they shouted. "Does God reject the very talent He has given to these gifted craftsmen and favor one who has little or nothing to offer?" Others argued that with such a paltry throne the Israelite God would appear less than those of the pagans.

Yielding to pressure, the high priest cast the die again. Again the choice fell upon Joseph's Ark. The crowd forced him to try for the third time. The result was the same. Amid their cries of protest God spoke up through a prophet standing in their midst.

"With a wondrous Ark," God said to the prophet, "My people may get lost in the beauty of their work. With a simple and humble Ark there will be nothing to distract them. Then they will think of me."

~ Moral ~

Give credit where it's ultimately due.

 Efficacious Prayer

If you want your prayer to be more efficacious,
don't perfect your prayer.
Perfect your love.

The Carnival

H E CAME TO THE CARNIVAL with high hopes and great expectations. There would be so much to do here, so much to experience. He had heard about it, all about it — about the breathtaking rides that whirled you and flipped you and raced you at eye-blurring speeds, about the exotic shows that titillated and excited you, and about the endless array of tantalizing foods.

The very air vibrated with the sounds of excitement and merriment. There was music from the carousel, screams from the roller coaster, clanging bells from the arcade, and hucksters everywhere barking their wares.

Exotic smells added to the enchantment. There was the burnt sugar allure of cotton candy, the deep-fried sweetness of powdered waffles, and the mouth-watering temptation of charcoal hot dogs.

And the people. People everywhere. Happy people. Exhausted people. Children scurrying from one attraction to another. Teenagers challenging and daring one another. Harried parents and tired old folks plodding wearily in search of an empty bench.

Yes, it was all he expected and more. After all, it was the carnival.

He was in a quandary about where to begin. Should he work his way up through the lesser attractions first, or go for broke right off? He decided to go for broke and try the rides first.

"You pays the price for the ride of your life," the barker challenged. It was the Whip. Terrifying. Tantalizing. Death-defying. "Only if you care to dare!" came the tempting warning.

The ride took him for all he was worth. With a whoosh it whipped him back against the padded seat. Faster than the speed of light it spun him, twirled him, and flipped him over and over. Then, as abruptly as it began, it came to a gut-wrenching stop. It took the breath right out of him and made rubber of his legs beneath him.

"Wow!"

He wobbled to the next attraction. Loop the Loop. It was mild by comparison. The Flipper was less yet and the Octopus was child's play. He had to go back to the Whip.

"You pays the price for the ride of your life."

He paid and rode it again. He tried to concentrate harder, experience it slower, but once again it was over lightning quick. He tried it again. And then again. And again and again.

He decided once more to try the other rides, but now they offered no comparison.

"Why go for less when we got the best?" the barker coaxed, pointing him back to the Whip. He returned, only with less anticipation and even less delight. He rode the Whip, disappointed that the other rides offered no alternative satisfaction and that the ultimate was now no longer enough. He would have to get out of this trap before he had no more money left.

Since the rides held no more attraction for him, he bought a hot dog and started down the midway.

"Tired of the merry-go-rounds, Sonny?" another barker asked. "Then come inside to a land of enchantment, a garden of Arabian delights, a sultan's private treasure. Exotic dancers straight from a sheik's harem. You pays the price for the thrill of your life."

There were new excitements to be found here. Different certainly from the sensation of being tossed about through space. Here the senses tingled. The body vibrated. Yet, it was not altogether unlike the Whip. Here too he lost his breath and his legs grew weak beneath him. Like the Whip, it too passed faster than the speed of light and returned him to the outside quicker than lightning.

After a few repeats, he moved on to some other midway attractions, but they seemed dull and boring by comparison.

"Why take less when we got the best?" another barker beckoned.

"Why, indeed?" he agreed.

Once again he was trapped. The ultimate had only left him hungry for more. But there was no more. Or was there?

"Through this door and you'll find what you're looking for," the next barker said, as if reading his thoughts.

"Is it better than the Whip?" he sneered.

"Better by a thousand times."

"Is it more exciting than the Sultan's Garden?"

"A paradise by comparison."

What could be greater than the dizzying thrill of the Whip? Than the sensual excitement of the Garden of Delights?

"Through this door," the barker teased, "there is delight beyond delights, joy beyond joys."

"Will it take my breath away?"

"That and more."

"Will it make my legs go rubbery?"

"It'll make your whole body go wobbily."

He could not resist. The temptation was too much.

"Through this door you'll find all that you're looking for and more. But only if you care and only if you dare."

"I care and I dare," he said fearfully, yet hopefully.

"First you pays your price. Then comes the thrill of your life."

The barker took all the money that he had left.

He passed through the door.

He was outside.

~ Moral ~

*There's more to get thrilled about in the ordinary
than the extraordinary.*

 ### The Solitary Life

*A bee cannot make honey without regularly going back
into the world to gather pollen.*

 ### Griping

Griping is adult whining.

 ### Vengeance

*You cannot walk through dung
without stinking up yourself.
It is better to walk around it
and let it lay there stinking by itself.*

20

Big Carrots and Little Carrots:
A Myth

O<small>N</small> M<small>OUNT</small> O<small>LYMPUS</small> an argument raged about the progress of humankind. The gods wanted to see humans make progress, but they disagreed on how it should be done.

Publicanus suggested that they throw a big carrot in front of them just out of reach. "Their desire for the carrot is all you need to move them," he said. "Then, when they have consumed that carrot, throw another one in front of them."

"It will require too many big carrots if that is what is required to move every person," they argued.

"No. That is the beauty of my plan. Place enough of an obstacle before them and it will require them to get the help of others. Then you need to throw only a few carrots to the most ambitious, the most greedy, the most aggressive and cleverest of people, and they will mobilize and organize the others to help them get it."

"Then what will the others get for their effort?"

"Little carrots."

"Why should they cooperate for such a paltry prize?"

"But they shall. They will be made to realize that without the drive and ingenuity of the ambitious they will get no carrots at all. In this way both are satisfied and progress takes place."

"Nay," said Demos. "One big carrot is enough to move all people to struggle together and share equally in the prize. Then when they have consumed that carrot, we throw another."

"That will not work," the other gods argued, "since humans are contentious creatures and will argue endlessly about the equal distribution of shares. They will become hopelessly mired in disputes and make no progress at all."

"The many will not and should not serve the few for less than equal shares," Demos contended. "They will not be swayed."

The gods could come to no decision. Therefore, the great god Zeus stepped into the breach. "Let humankind be given both options and make their own choice."

So it happened and the debate has raged among humans ever since.

 Splitting Hairs

The history of the world has taught us that all too often splitting hairs ends up in splitting heads.

21

The Enchanted Bird

ONCE UPON A TIME there was a beautiful princess who lived in a magnificent castle in the midst of an enchanted forest. One day as she strolled idly along a wooded path she suddenly became captivated by a bird's wondrous singing. Never before had she heard anything so sweet and so heart-rending as to instantly bring joy to her heart and tears to her eyes. She scanned the canopy that spread umbrella-like over her, but she couldn't find where the music was coming from. She ran from arbor to arbor listening closely and searching carefully, frightened that the bird might fly away and she'd never discover what it was that had given her such intense joy.

At long last, just before sunset she saw the bird light upon the topmost branch of a stately hemlock. The sight of it was even more wonderful than its haunting music. The bird was not only a banquet for the ears but a feast for the eyes. Truly, this was an enchanted bird. The princess felt at once that she must have it.

She stalked the enchanted bird for days on end until finally she was able to trap and capture it. However, no sooner did she secure it to a perch than it bit through its bonds and flew away, free once again. This first attempt had taken so much effort she knew that a repeated attempt would require additional help.

So the princess went to a bold and daring young prince and told him of her quest. When he too saw the magnificent bird and heard its song, he knew that he could not live without it either. So together they set out to catch the enchanted bird.

With two of them in pursuit they were able to capture it in short order. Once again when it was tied to a perch, it bit through its bonds and flew away. Try as they might they could find no way to keep the enchanted bird captive. In the end they decided to explain their plight to the palace sorcerer.

To their astonishment they discovered he had an identical bird inside his hut. However, it was neither caged nor tethered. It actually flew free. But, amazingly, it never seemed to leave the wizard's side.

"How is it," they asked the wizard, "that we cannot hold ours captive and yours will not leave you?"

"The answer, my young friends, is quite simple," he said. "The enchanted bird is very powerful, as you have discovered. There is no way on earth that it can be held captive. But, as you can see, once you've discovered its secret, it will never leave you."

"What is its secret?" they asked excitedly.

"The secret, my children, is really not very secret at all. You want the bird for your sake. That will never work. You must want the bird for its sake. You must do for the bird what *it* wants and it will never leave you."

"What do you mean?" they asked innocently.

"It is not what you want but what the bird needs that will make it stay with you. Discover this and it will be your friend for life."

"What does the bird need?"

"That no one can tell you. That you must learn for yourselves," he said wisely.

The next day the prince and the princess followed the bird everywhere it went in order to discover what it was that the bird needed. The bird led them on a merry chase over hill and through dale but they could discover nothing. Each night the bird, weakened by its busy daily excursion, would slowly make its way to a perch atop a high mountain and collapse. Each morning as the sun rose the bird would straighten itself to full stature and bask in its invigorating rays. Its colors would brighten and its voice would gain strength. Then it would fly off through the forest showing its beauty and sharing its song with all in the valley.

"It's the sun!" they cried. "The enchanted bird needs the sun."

So the princess and the prince brought the sun into their lives by getting married and loving each other, everyone, and everything. The enchanted bird moved into the castle with them where it found the nourishment and strength it needed to continue singing its sweet song to those in the castle and throughout the kingdom. And they all lived happily ever after.

~ Moral ~

Love needs God.

 Time Well Spent

Don't waste your time trying to get people to love you.
Instead, spend your time loving people
and the other will follow.

A Tale of Two Flowers

ONCE UPON A TIME there were two flowers. One was bright yellow and the other bright blue. From the very first instant they opened their face to the world, the world heaped profuse praise upon them for their vigor and their beauty.

"I love your face," said the sun to the yellow flower, who blazed at the compliment.

"I love your eyes," said the sky to the blue flower, who swooned in excitement.

"I love your beauty," said the butterfly. "And I love your pollen," said the bee. "I love your nectar," said the ant. "I, your shade," said the grasshopper. Everyone and everything lavished endless praises upon them.

The flowers basked in the accolades. It was exhilarating. "Never stop!" they said to the world.

The next day the yellow flower got busy working.

"What are you doing?" asked the blue flower.

"Making pollen," she replied.

"You really shouldn't, you know," said the blue flower. It'll make you look old before your time." The yellow flower paid no attention and continued with her work.

The following day, the world again complimented the blue flower but said nothing to the yellow flower, who looked a little wrinkled and worn.

"What did I tell you," said the blue flower. "You must direct all your efforts at keeping yourself beautiful or no one will notice you anymore. She primped her petals and primed her color. In time she worked just as hard to stay pretty as the yellow flower did to make pollen. Only everyone complimented her and no one noticed her friend anymore.

Then one day a man came into the garden and marveled at the beauty of the blue flower. "This one I must take to my house," he exclaimed.

"What did I tell you?" the blue flower said to the yellow flower. "Now I will adorn someone's house while you remain out here to wither away." The yellow flower for her part said nothing.

In time when the man was finished with the blue flower he cast it away. In time when nature was finished with the yellow flower there was a whole field full of yellow blossoms.

 Old Folks, Old Flowers

Old people like old flowers are supposed to go to seed.
If they expend all their energy trying to remain flowers,
they have nothing to give the future.

~ 23 ~

The Game

IN A VAST FIELD that stretched farther than the eye can see, a great multitude of people milled about as if waiting for something to happen. At long last a messenger came into their midst bearing important news.

"You are to walk around this field twenty-five times carrying this baton," he proclaimed, holding aloft a round stick.

"And when we have done so what will happen at the end?" one of the crowd asked.

"You will learn that when you have finished," he said and left.

So the great crowd ambled off to make its first circuit of the vast field. Sometimes the adults carried the baton. Sometimes the children carried it . . . and played with it. Sometimes the people hurried and sometimes they just meandered along. Day followed day as they slowly but steadily made their way around the field. After a considerably long period they completed the first circuit. A celebration was held to commemorate the event and a good time was had by *all*.

During the festivities someone suggested that "just for the hell of it" they could make the next trip around the field more interesting by dividing themselves up into teams and racing against one other. This seemed like a good idea. It would give a whole new dimension to what could otherwise become a monotonous routine. In no time at all almost everyone was persuaded to go along, so they broke themselves up into Red, Yellow, Brown, Black, and White teams. However, there were some who refused to go along so they were called the Others. The strange thing was that they were given the baton to carry since the racing teams argued and couldn't agree upon which one of them should carry it. Instead they decided that each team should make and carry its own baton. The Red Team made a red baton, the Yellow Team a yellow baton, and so on.

All the teams then got on their mark, got set, and took off at breakneck speed. All the teams, that is, except the Others, who set out in the same way they had *all* done before. As far as the racing teams were concerned the Others were out of it. Even though they all worked hard, the field was still vast and took a great deal of time to get around. At the completion of this circuit the Yellow Team won. The Yellow Team celebrated *its* victory with a great deal of fanfare while the losing teams sulked and challenged them to another try.

"Why not?" they all agreed. "Since we still have twenty-three more circuits to go."

Then someone suggested that "just for the hell of it" at certain agreed upon places around the field they might leave a group of runners so that the next time around the field they could just pass the baton along from group to group. This would save them from having everybody run around the field each time. Thus the first relay race was born.

As the teams raced around they left small groups of runners behind for the next race. The Black Team won this race and the White Team won the first relay race. In the meantime the Others just continued to make their way around the field. But not nearly as quickly as the racing teams, who literally left them in the dust.

After a while the competition got very intense. It wasn't long before the racing teams realized that the slow runners were holding them back, so they decided that only the strong and the fast would be allowed to compete. The slow and the weak were simply left in the field to do as they wished. But they were no longer in the game.

A few more relays were held, and sometimes the same team won and sometimes different teams won. This brought them to a new observation. Some teams were being held back because of their slower runners. So someone suggested that "just for the hell of it" they race individual runners against one another rather than team against team. The Yellow Team put forth its best runner, the Brown Team its best runner, and so on.

When the Brown runner won the first individual race and celebrated *his* victory the other runners on the Brown Team became jealous and wanted to race against him so that they could run in the next circuit. The same thing happened with all the other teams too. Before long, the teams faded into the background until they were left with only individuals racing against individuals.

In the meantime the Others continued to plod their way around the field circuit after circuit until they completed all twenty-five of them. When it was done they all threw a marvelous celebration where there was feasting and dancing.

When the messenger came and joined the party, they said to him, "When we asked you what would happen after we circled the field twenty-five times you said that we would learn the answer when we finished. Well, we've finished. What is it?"

"That you made it," he said simply.

They were stunned. Is that all there was to it? They had made this long journey simply to be able to say that they had made it. Yet, when they thought about it, they realized that he was right. They had made it. That's what they were all so happy about, wasn't it? Wasn't that what they were all celebrating?

"But what about the others?" they asked, looking around and seeing that none of the others had arrived.

"The others?" the messenger said looking sad. "As you can see they didn't make it. And that's the hell of it."

~ Moral ~

Life is a game we can't make it through alone.

 ## Competition

*Winning races doesn't build character
as much as losing them does.*

 ## The Cutting Edge

*You don't have to go anywhere
to be at the cutting edge of life.
There is need everywhere.
The cutting edge is wherever you want to start cutting.*

 ## Jealousy

*Jealous people are stingy people.
Be generous with your love
and you will never be jealous.*

~ 24 ~

Hair Spray

SHE HAD BEEN combing and styling her hair for what seemed like hours. Her hair was her pride and joy. It was long and blond and wavy. There was a luster and beauty to it that everyone couldn't help but notice. Each way she combed it looked better than the last. Each way she styled it was more attractive than ever. It was impossible for it not to look good. It was almost impossible to decide on a style.

At last, she did. Every hair was in place and the look of it was remarkably beautiful. Then came the final step. She must spray it so that it would stay exactly that way throughout the day. She sprayed profusely until the entire coiffure was locked in immobility.

The morning rain could not wilt it. The afternoon activity did not ruffle it. The evening breeze failed to dishevel it.

It was still in perfect shape at the after-theater cocktail party when she overheard someway say, "Too bad she couldn't do as much with her face."

~ Moral ~

All is vanity.

~ 25 ~

Heaven's Gate

ONCE UPON A TIME, at the edge of a very large forest there lived a woodsman and his son. He was a good and hardworking man who had permission from the king to cut all the wood that was needed in the castle for building, or for furniture, or for fuel and to take whatever wood was necessary to provide for himself and his family. He worked hard, but he made a good living and sincerely wished for his son to follow in his footsteps. The boy, however, would have none of it. He considered his father's work much too strenuous and difficult and preferred to find some easier livelihood, like hunting. A royal gamekeeper would always have enough to eat and for just a minimum amount of effort. It wasn't that he was lazy. He simply saw no benefit in stressing himself and suffering when he didn't have to.

One day while the boy was out tramping about in the woods, he quite accidently stumbled upon an old hermit's cabin. Although the hermit was well known throughout the region because of the many kind deeds he continually did for the poor and unfortunate peasants, no one knew precisely where he lived. The holy man just seemed to emerge from the forest, do his good deed, and disappear back into the woods. This explains why he was so startled when he heard a knocking on his door. He greeted the young man with all due Christian courtesy and invited him in. He could not have treated him better if the young man were the good Lord Jesus Himself, which is the way all holy persons treat strangers.

After he had eaten, the boy listened attentively all afternoon and evening as the old man told him stories of great men and women who did wonderful deeds and were now saints in heaven. Before leaving he begged the hermit to allow him to return and hear more of his stories. The hermit agreed provided that he promise not to tell anyone where he lived.

Throughout the summer and into fall the young man visited the hermit regularly. The holy man would feed him from his simple larder and tell him stories about the great saints of heaven.

Then one day the boy asked, "What do you do when I'm not here?" He was seriously wondering if becoming a hermit would be a worthwhile pursuit for him.

"Oh, I help out here and there," he answered.

"Doing what?" the young man continued more curious than ever.

"Sometimes I help an overburdened farmer cut his hay. Sometimes I gather nuts and berries to bring to a poor family. Sometimes I help a man gather twigs or a woman haul water. I even occasionally help animals who get hurt or into trouble. I am grateful for whatever work the Lord sends me each day. I want no thanks for it, which is why I want no one to know where I live."

"Is it hard work, would you say?" the boy asked.

"I would say it is oftentimes difficult, especially since I am not proficient in any trade that would make some tasks I do easier. I struggle along as best I can."

Struggle was not to the young man's liking so he decided that being a hermit was not in his future. He again thought about becoming a royal gamekeeper.

When the first heavy snow of winter fell, the old hermit bid the young man farewell. The boy asked if he was going somewhere.

"A trip to somewhere," he said. "I hope you will eventually follow me. But before I go I have something I wish to give you." The old man opened the trunk at the foot of his bed and took out a knife. There was nothing extravagant or special about the knife except that it was exceedingly sharp. Then the hermit said a strange thing. "One day this may open heaven's gate for you." After that the boy never saw the hermit again.

When he got home he spent many idle winter hours whittling away with his knife. The blade was indeed so sharp that it cut through even the hardest wood as if it were soft butter. By winter's end the young man knew exactly what he would do with the rest of his life. Over the months he had carved a statue of the old hermit that was so delicate and life-like and so easy to do that he decided that he would be a wood carver. He would carve magnificent statues of all the great men and women the hermit had told him about.

Thus it was that the woodsman's son became a woodcarver and spent his entire life effortlessly carving statues of the saints, the blessed Virgin, and Jesus crucified. When he was getting on in years he decided to accomplish one final masterpiece — a work that would open heaven's gate for him. He began carving an entire church out of wood. The knife literally flew in his hands. The fluted columns, the ornate cornices, the delicate lattice work, the life-sized statues over the altars, the filigreed pulpit, and the inlaid altar combined to make the work a monumental masterpiece.

The woodcarver had no sooner finished when he died. He approached heaven's gate with a light and happy heart. The gate was closed. He pushed against it fully expecting it to swing wide open, but it didn't. He tried again with all his might, which wasn't much since he never really exerted himself on earth. Nonetheless, it should have been sufficient to open the gate, but it didn't. Then he remembered what the holy hermit told him. The knife would open heaven's gate for him. He thought of inserting the knife into the key hole, only there was none. He tried cutting through the ornate doors but for the first time the knife failed him. He screamed out in anger and anguish. It did no good. The gate remained closed to him.

Not knowing what to do, he decided to return to earth again. When he arrived it was the dead of winter. A heavy snowstorm was blanketing the area in a way he had never seen before. The peasants of the forest and the village all gathered in the woodcarver's church. A tall, strong-looking peasant ascended the pulpit steps.

"If we remain here, we may survive this storm," he said solemnly. "There is not enough wood to heat all our homes separately. Let us bring all the firewood we have left and heat the church."

When the people returned there was only enough wood to last two days at the most. The storm continued into the third day. Again someone ascended the pulpit and said, "We must cut down trees or we shall all freeze to death."

"What shall we cut them with? Our fingers?" the crowd responded. "Only the royal woodsmen have axes and they are far from here. If someone tries to reach them he will certainly die before he gets there."

"Then there is no hope," the man in the pulpit said.

A grim silence filled the church. At long last, the woodcarver spoke up. No one acted surprised to see him since no one had yet discovered that he died. "There is a way," he said. Taking the hermit's knife he cut off the extended arm of St. Michael the Archangel. The peasants gasped. "I'm sure St. Michael doesn't mind giving his arm in a good cause." Although the woodcarver smiled his heart was breaking over the destruction of one of his masterpieces. When he cut off the other arm it hurt as much as if he were cutting off his own.

All through the night and into the next few days, the woodcarver dissected all his great works until nothing was left. The statues, the pulpit, the altars, the columns, even the great crucifix had all been sacrificed. Never had the poor woodcarver experienced such pain and suffering. There was nothing left for the world to remember him by. Not a thing. It had all been for nothing.

Except that the peasants had survived the storm. What was left of the church was a shambles never again able to be rebuilt.

After the last peasant left the woodcarver cried over the destruction of his life's work. The tears poured out in a steady flood as he staggered down the aisle to the front door of the church. He was about to push it open when he heard singing outside. The music was so unexpected and so heavenly that he just stood there listening for a long while. Then he realized that he was no longer standing before the church door. He was at heaven's gate.

Just the slightest touch and it opened effortlessly. Standing within was the holy hermit surrounded by all the great saints whose statues he had carved. The woodcarver could think of nothing else to say but "Why?"

It was no longer the hermit but Jesus Himself who smiled warmly at him. "Heaven's gate," he said, "is opened only through suffering."

 Pettiness

*People who can't see the big picture pick away
at the little one until there's nothing left.*

~ 26 ~

The Iron Ring

ONCE UPON A TIME the wicked witch of Terron became terribly upset and angry because she wasn't invited to the young prince's first birthday party. All the other notables of the kingdom received invitations from the king and queen, but not the witch. For such an affront to her dignity she vowed to take her revenge out on the child. Because of this the royal couple decreed that the prince should never be more than a few arms' length from a circle of royal guardsmen.

Day and night the child was surrounded by his protectors. The witch could not approach to cause any harm but neither could the child be free to do the things of childhood. This in itself was a curse, but the king and queen failed to see it because they only wanted to protect their son.

This presented only minor difficulties when he was a child, as children adapt most readily even to the most difficult of environments. But what adolescent wants to be encircled day and night by a phalanx of overzealous soldiers watching his every move? So he devised a plan for how he might get free.

The next day while he was swimming in the river surrounded again by the usual cadre of soldiers, he took a deep breath and submerged under the water. He swam a very long distance until he thought his lungs would burst before he surfaced again. It had worked. He was all alone. For the first time that he could remember he was completely alone with no one around him, no one watching him. At first he felt strangely isolated and afraid. Then he thought about his freedom and romped excitedly through the woods like a wild young stag.

When he eventually tired from all his frolicking he collapsed happily in the high grass. He knew that any moment now the soldiers would find him and his new-found freedom would be over.

But it wasn't the soldiers who found him. It was the witch.

"Tired, my young stag?" she said.

"Tired, but happy," the prince answered.

"Why are you happy?" she asked.

"Because for once in my life I am not surrounded by my body-guards. For once in my life I'm free. That's why I'm happy."

"Why should you be happy when I have been affronted? I was to have laid a curse on you for not being invited to your first birthday party. But I didn't have to bother since the one your father imposed on you was worse than any I might have devised. Only now you have discovered a way to get around it, so I must lay my own upon you. What was to be your protection will now be your curse."

The witch took an iron ring from her finger and stretched it to the point where it could go no farther without breaking, about three paces across. She threw this around the young man.

"Henceforth," she said, "if you set foot outside this ring of iron you shall die."

The young prince was dumbfounded. He had forgotten about the witch and her anger in spite of his parents' warnings. Now his folly would cost him dearly. He tried to plead with her.

"Please. Have pity on me."

"Pity," she laughed. "There is no pity, no warmth in the heart of a witch."

At that moment the soldiers appeared and the witch disappeared. The young prince thought this must have been just a bad dream. When he went to follow his bodyguard back to the castle he stepped over the ring. He immediately collapsed, struggling desperately to breathe. He was just barely able to crawl back into the ring.

The news of the prince's terrible plight spread throughout the kingdom. People came from everywhere to offer their condolences and advice. But nothing worked. Every time the prince tried to leave the ring of iron he was unable to breathe. He was doomed to be a prisoner of the ring for the rest of his life. Only the old hermit of the woods offered some hope.

"Evil cannot prevail," he said. "Every curse must have within it its own undoing. Of that you may be sure, for God has willed it so."

But there was apparently no undoing of this curse, for the best minds of the kingdom had tried and failed. The prince lived in the ring of iron trapped as its prisoner. In frustration he tried breaking it, for it was very thin. But he couldn't. Nor could anyone else. So wherever he went he would have to carry the ring with him.

At first everyone did what they could for the prince. Playmates and friends would enter the circle to keep him company. But they soon felt too confined to remain very long. Then the prince became demanding. This had to be brought to him and that had to come to him. Since he couldn't get out, he tried to force everything to come into his own little world. The more demanding and selfish he became, the more others resented and avoided him. They stayed far away because that he couldn't make demands on them if he couldn't see them and they couldn't hear him. He was alone, lonely, and miserable. The curse was working its full power on him.

One day as the prince sat in his iron circle at the edge of the royal gardens a peasant girl picking berries came upon him. Since she was not of the royal court she had no idea who he was. She offered him some of her berries. It had been so long since anyone had approached him willingly and kindly that the prince didn't know how to act. The girl took his silence to mean that he wasn't interested and started walking away. The prince couldn't bear the idea of being alone anymore and called out to her.

"Please don't go. I would love some of your berries."

She came back and sat with him conversing and eating berries. Each day she returned and spent time with the young prince. In time when they became friends the prince told her who he was and about the terrible curse he was living under. Instead of being frightened away the girl came and spent more time with him. After a while they fell deeply in love with one another.

However, this only made the prince's plight worse than it already was. How could he ask her to marry him and spend the rest of her life confined to his ring of iron? When she told him that true love will always find a way, he remembered the words of the old hermit that every curse has within itself its own undoing.

The prince wondered how it might apply to him. When he realized that he could not bring the girl he loved and her world into the circle with him, the question became how to make his circle bigger and go out to them? How indeed?

The answer was somewhere in what the girl and the hermit had said. He had somehow to put the two together. Finally, it occurred to him.

He asked his love to stand outside the ring of iron. He stood there looking at her with all the love in his heart. There is no warmth in the heart of a witch, but there is in a heart filled with love. The warmth of his love had softened the iron. He stretched the ring out to include her. When she realized what he was doing, she too began to look at the world around them with great love. Again the ring became pliant and was stretched to include more of the world around them. The more they loved the more the ring of iron spread until it encircled the entire kingdom.

The prince was no longer a prisoner. He and love had undone the curse. So the prince married his true love and they lived happily, but not ever after. They knew that wouldn't happen until their love stretched the ring until it was no more.

~ 27 ~

Radishes

THERE ONCE WAS A MAN who had an uncontrollable appetite for radishes. He devoured radishes whenever and wherever he could. Because his passion for radishes was costing him a great deal of money as the price of them kept increasing, he decided that he would grow his own radishes.

So he went to the store and asked the storekeeper if he had radish seeds.

"No, I don't," the man said. "But I do have squash seeds."

The man bought the squash seeds and went home and planted them. He cultivated the ground, removed unwanted stones and weeds, dug furrows, and carefully planted the seeds. He took special care of the plants as they grew, watering, fertilizing, and weeding his garden. Finally, they grew into full-fledged squash.

But the man did not want squash. He wanted radishes. He went to the shopkeeper and vented his anger.

"I told you they were squash seeds," the shopkeeper replied.

"Well, I don't want squash. I want radishes. Do you have any radish seeds?"

"No, I don't," the man told him. "But I do have pumpkin seeds."

So the man bought the pumpkin seeds and went home and planted pumpkin seeds in his garden. He carefully cultivated the ground, removed unwanted stones and weeds, dug deep furrows, and placed the seeds in them. As they grew he watered, fertilized, and weeded the garden. At last, it yielded beautiful pumpkins.

But he did not want pumpkins. He wanted radishes. He went back to the shopkeeper and complained bitterly.

"I told you they were pumpkin seeds," he said. "I don't have radish seeds."

"What kind of seeds do you have?" the man asked again.

"I have some watermelon seeds."

So the man bought the watermelon seeds and took them home with him. Once again he carefully tilled the soil in his garden, removed unwanted stones and weeds, dug deep furrows, and placed the watermelon seeds in them. As the plants took root and grew he watered, fertilized, and weeded the garden. Finally, it yielded nice, plump watermelons.

But the man did not want watermelons. This time he did not go back to the shopkeeper. Instead he just raged and raged and swore that he would never go back to him again.

~ Moral ~

If you don't like what you've been growing,
ask yourself what you've been sowing.

 Fleas

A man's house was so full of annoying fleas
that he decided to get rid of them once and for all.
So he burned down his house.

~ 28 ~

Squire John

ONCE UPON A TIME there was a young man named John. He was a squire in the castle of King Arthur. He worked hard and did all that squires have to do if they want to become knights one day. Squire John certainly hoped to become a knight, but secretly he hoped to be one of the famous and gallant knights of the Round Table. He felt certain that if he worked very hard his dream would come true.

Every year at harvest time there would be a great tournament. All the knights of the realm would assemble and take part in the exciting jousting matches. This was to be Squire John's first time at the event, since he had just begun his apprenticeship. He was even more excited than all the others who had come from far and wide to attend the great spectacle. Squire John joined the noisy ranks of the crowd watching as the gallant knights made their way onto the field. They were met with thunderous cheers and applause. They were all fine and noble looking men, especially those of the Round Table.

Then a strange thing happened. When the last knight entered the arena, the crowd did not cheer or shout. Instead, they fell into a deep silence. It was as if the entire assembly was holding its breath. Squire John looked to see what was the cause of this strange reaction. It was Sir Lancelot. Immediately, the young man knew why the crowd became hushed. Lancelot was breathtakingly handsome. He was more beautiful than any person Squire John had ever seen. Seeing Lancelot mounted on his horse in full armor in the brilliant sunlight, the boy thought that the very sun itself had come down into their midst. He said to himself, "Oh, if only I could be breathtakingly handsome like that!"

Once Squire John set eyes on this legendary hero he knew that he could never be content again with just his ordinary ambition. Becoming a knight would not be enough. Becoming a knight of the Round Table would not be enough. More than anything in the whole world he wanted to be as handsome as the magnificent Sir Lancelot. Unfortunately, however, he was intelligent enough to know that nature had not treated him very kindly when it came to looks. One is either born to beauty or he is not. Squire John was not. He was more than just plain. He was homely.

He was not dismayed, however. There was still hope for him in the person of Merlin the Magician. He found the wizard in the castle tower bent over his boiling cauldron.

"What is it you wish of me?" Merlin asked.

"A wish is precisely what I have come about," Squire John answered.

"Tell me what it is?" The magician never looked up at him. He just kept stirring his pot.

"I know that what I will ask of you will sound vain and foolish, but I promise that if you grant me my wish I will use it wisely."

"Ask," Merlin said getting a bit impatient.

Squire John swallowed deeply and blurted out, "I wish to be handsome." There! He said it and he meant it, even if he was embarrassed because of it.

"Not an unusual request," the magician said.

"Ca...ca...can you grant my wish?" he stammered nervously.

"I can satisfy your need," Merlin said.

Squire John grinned from ear to ear. "If you can grant me my wish, I promise I will do anything and everything I can in payment for it."

It would be well worth it, he thought, in order to become one of the handsomest men in the kingdom.

"As I said," Merlin continued. "I can satisfy your need. But there are two conditions."

"Name them. Just name them," Squire John said, "and I will fulfill them."

"First, you must become my apprentice. And, second, you may not look at your face again until you are ready. Do you accept these conditions?"

Squire John was troubled. How long would he have to work for the magician? How long would he have to wait to become handsome?

"How long must I wait?" he asked.

"Until you are ready," the wily old sorcerer answered.

Well, I will hurry up and make myself ready as soon as possible, the boy thought. Then I will be handsome. And finally I will become a knight.

"I accept," he said.

Squire John immediately began his apprenticeship under Merlin the Magician. Over the months and years he carefully learned all that the wise sorcerer taught him. As he did he moved out of the castle more and more to work the wonders of Merlin's magic and wisdom among the people. As he grew more skilled he became increasingly more beloved to those whom he served. Yet whenever he would ask the crafty magician when he could once again look upon his face he was told that he could not until the time was right. He had never once betrayed his word. From the day he promised he never again looked at his image, either in a mirror, or a reflecting pond, or in a brass plate. He did all that he had promised and more because he was indeed an honorable young man.

One day as Squire John was making his way back to the king's castle after helping some poor peasants in the country, he heard a great commotion. The sound was unmistakable. He had forgotten that it was the harvest season and that the annual tournament was about to take place. He made his way hurriedly to the jousting field to see the pageantry and also to catch another glimpse of that most handsome knight whom he had not seen since that fateful day he first set eyes upon him. The cheers and shouts were getting louder as he approached. Then just as he remembered long ago, the crowd fell into a hushed and profound silence. John looked to see where Lancelot was. He couldn't find him. He turned round and round, but Lancelot wasn't there. Then why was the crowd so silent? He looked around. All eyes were on him.

"It's me!" he thought. "They're looking at me!"

The time had come. Just as Merlin had said. The time was right and the crowd was staring at him the way they once did at Lancelot. He must be very handsome indeed for them to react this way. He wanted to shout out, loudly as he could, but that would not have been gentlemanly. So he shouted it to himself. "At last! I'm handsome. At last, I'm handsome."

Now he yearned to see exactly what he looked like. But he must thank Merlin first for what he had done. He raced up the tower stairs and burst into the magician's room. Merlin was not there. He was dumbstruck. He did not expect this. Merlin had never not been there ever before. His cauldron hung in the fireplace as usual but it was not boiling and he was not hovering nearby.

Squire John called out, but there was no answer. He looked around frantically. There was a note on the table. "The time is right," it said. "Look into the pot."

Squire John carefully peered into the pot. The dark liquid was like a mirror. For the first time in years he was about to see his face. He braced himself and took a deep breath. At first he was startled. Then he smiled. Finally, he laughed uproariously. It was a deep and hearty laugh.

The carefully chosen words of the wily wizard now came back to him. *"I can satisfy your need,"* he said. "I can satisfy your need," not, "I will grant your wish." In truth, he had satisfied a young man's heartfelt need, but not his frivolous wish. It was the same face. The same face, only older and wiser.

Squire John never became a knight. It didn't interest him anymore. And with Merlin gone, he was busier and happier than ever. Besides who ever heard of a sorcerer with a pretty face?

 Time to Waste

"Come stir the water with me, today,"
said the child to the old man.
"I must not," said the old man,
"for I am not so sure of tomorrow."

 Dressing for Life

The first and primary reason for clothes is protection.
Then, modesty. And finally, fashion.
We don't wear high fashion to the steel plant.
Nor can you wear unrestrained individualism
in the world.
Periodically, life calls us back to the essentials.

~ 29 ~

The Stick

EARLY ONE SPRING a boy began a hike up a mountainside. His father suggested that he should have a walking stick. He searched and found one that was just the right size and shape. Since he wasn't quite sure how to use it, it was more a playful distraction than a practical help. It wasn't until he was exhausted and couldn't scale a difficult rocky ledge and his father told him to extend the stick so that he could pull him up that he realized that the stick actually had a practical value. Its value grew still when he learned to use it to push aside thorny brush or to ward off bothersome snakes.

When they came off the mountain the boy took the stick home with him. He learned that he could while away the hours by using it as a bat to hit anything from baseballs to stones, a sword to fight off evil knights, and even a Samurai weapon.

One day he distractedly left the stick on the ground after a long bout of play. A gang of thugs found it and took it off with them. In a fight with a rival gang it was used to inflict many an injury on a number of belligerent opponents.

During the summer it had become a formidable weapon indeed. In one violent confrontation it was wrenched away and hurled into a nearby creek. It floated downstream to a lake where the wind and the waves cleaned off the grime, smoothed its surface, and left it gleaming white on the shore. An old man hobbled by and found the stick ideal for a cane, so he took it with him to his cabin in the woods. Throughout the remainder of the autumn and into the winter it was an invaluable assistance wherever he went.

Then during an especially cold and stormy winter night the old man threw the stick into the fire, and before it ended its long sojourn it gave him comforting heat.

~ Moral ~

Life is what you make it.

 Say Something New

When it comes to wisdom nothing we say is new.
Only the way we say it is.

~ 30 ~

Strength

A YOUNG MAN exercised for long hours over many difficult days to make his body firm and his muscles hard. When he was finished his body was like a rock. He came before his mentor.

"I am strong now!" he said to his teacher.

The master took a stone and with the swift blow of a mallet shattered it to pieces.

"What have you learned?" he asked.

"The rock was strong," replied the boy, "but the mallet was stronger still."

"You have answered correctly," said the master. He then swung the mallet against a piece of cloth. "What have you learned now?"

"The cloth though softer was stronger than the mallet."

The master took scissors and cut the cloth. "And now?"

"What is sharp is stronger than what is soft."

The master took the scissors to the lake and cut the water.

"What have you learned now?"

"What is fluid is stronger than what is sharp."

The master put some water in a container and boiled it over a fire until there was nothing left.

"Speak!" said the master.

The boy said, "What is hot is greater than what is liquid."

The master then threw a rock, the mallet, the cloth, the scissors, the water, and the fire into the air.

"What have you learned my firm young man."

"I have learned master that what is not seen is the strongest of all."

That said, the master left.

 ## Show Offs

Young people like to show off their bodies.
But is that not what flowers are about?

 ## Values

If you're fifty and you look thirty,
you've spent entirely too much time on your body.

The Strange Land of Yet:
A Story of Adolescence

ONCE UPON A TIME there was a boy named Jimmy Jumper.
Oh! How he loved to jump. He would jump over fences, over rocks,
over bushes, over everything. Sometimes he jumped into things he
couldn't jump out of. He should have known that. I mean if you
jump into a lake, you can't jump out of it again. That's why people
say, "Look before you leap."

Well, this time Jimmy really did it. He jumped over a bush without
looking and fell down a deep, deep hole. There's no telling how long
he fell because he wasn't wearing a watch; and he couldn't tell where he
had fallen because he didn't have a compass. One thing he did know
was that he had come upon a strange place. He knew that because he
had a brain and he did bring that with him. Besides, once he got on
his feet and walked a few paces he saw a sign that read: Welcome to
the Strange Land of Yet.

Jimmy no sooner read the sign when two soldiers grabbed him
under the arms and carried him off. "What a fine welcome this is!"
he thought. They dumped him unceremoniously at the feet of a king
seated on his throne. He was the worst-dressed king Jimmy had ever
seen. His clothes looked like they had come straight from a garbage

can. His shoes looked as if they had been put through a meat grinder. He wore only one sock and that had lost its elastic so it was wrapped around his ankle. His pants were hopelessly tattered and torn. His grimy shirt was hanging out. His nose was running and his greasy hair hadn't been combed in months if not years.

"All hail, King Shoddy!" the soldiers said and hurried away.

"What's this? What's this?" the king said, wiping his nose on his sleeve. "What have we here?"

"I'm a boy. Can't you tell?" Once again Jimmy jumped right in without looking.

"A boy is it? Yes! Yes! I can see that," King Shoddy said, singing the words like a lullaby. Then, just as quick as summer lightning, he pointed a long bony finger with a red nail at him and screamed, "I CAN CHANGE YOU INTO A SNIVELING SNAKE IF I'VE A MIND TO. DON'T TAMPER WITH ME, BOY!"

Jimmy almost fell over, the king startled him so. Startled but not frightened. "Listen," he said finding his courage. "I didn't ask to come here. I stumbled into this place, and I'd just as soon get out of here."

King Shoddy slouched back on his throne, stretching his long legs in front of him. He looked down his running nose at Jimmy. "You didn't stumble into this place, boy" he sneered. "You jumped into it." Jimmy squirmed a little bit. The king saw this momentary weakness and attacked. "And there's no jumping out, either!"

"Well, I won't stay," Jimmy said, stamping his foot on the ground.

The king's wizard suddenly appeared. Appropriately enough, the wizard was dressed as shabbily as the king. He leaned over and whispered into the king's ear, "You can't keep him you know. It's against the rules."

The king waved the wizard away and peered down his nose at the boy. "Let's not be at odds with one another," he purred soothingly. "This is a wonderful place to be and the people are not half bad, given the chance. Since you're going to be with us for a while, why not make yourself comfortable?"

The king stepped down from his throne slowly and deliberately. He reached out an arm and placed it around Jimmy's shoulders. The gesture felt warm and assuring. "Stay wherever you like as long as you want," he said.

"Thanks," Jimmy said. "But I want to go back."

The king withdrew his arm as if he had been stung by a bee and screamed at the top of his voice, "THERE'S NO GOING BACK, BOY!" The wizard made a move to approach the king again, but the king saw him coming and waved him away. He lowered his voice and continued. "As I said, we're not half bad once you've been here for a while. Take your time."

Jimmy was too confused to understand what was happening to him. "Where will I go?" he asked.

"Wherever you wish," the king replied.

"What will I do?"

"Whatever you like."

"How long do I have to be here?"

"As long as you want," the king smiled agreeably. "There! You see how accommodating we are."

"If what you say is true, then this place isn't half bad at that."

"Stick with us, boy. You ain't seen nothin' yet," the king leered.

Well, Jimmy was curious about this strange place and since he did jump into it he might as well take the time to see what it was like. If he didn't like it, he could always go back. He didn't half believe the king anyway.

"I'll stay!" Jimmy said. "At least for a while."

"Good," said the king, turning away from the boy. As he ascended the steps to his throne without bothering to look back at him, he added, "I'll see that you're taken care of."

Just ahead of him, Jimmy saw flashing lights. As he cautiously drew closer he saw that it was a spectacular lightning storm. But it wasn't exactly a storm either since there was no thunder and no rain. It was just a giant light display. Lightning flashed everywhere, and without the usual accompaniments he found that he wasn't the least bit afraid. In fact, he was intrigued. He was about to step into it, when something fell out of the sky right smack in front of him.

It was the most amazing creature Jimmy had ever seen. Everything about him was blue. Everything he wore was blue from his shirt to his shoes. His hair, face, hands, and even his fingernails were blue.

"What are you?" Jimmy asked. This was certainly a strange but interesting place, Jimmy thought.

"I'm a Crony," he said.

"Where did you come from?"

"Out of the blue."

"Are you putting me on?" Jimmy glowered.

"No. But you can put me on," he said.

"What's that supposed to mean?" This Crony seemed a little too clever, too cool to Jimmy. He was used to doing it to others but not having it done to him.

"Were you sent by King Shoddy to take care of me?"

"Heavens, no!" said the Crony.

"Then what are you doing here?"

"I've come to take care of you."

There he was doing it again. "Are you sure you're not putting me on?" Jimmy frowned.

"I couldn't even if I wanted to," he said. "It doesn't work that way."

"What are you talking about?"

Suddenly, the lightning started flashing brighter and more often. Jimmy was amazed that he could see the lightning streaks in a daytime sky. The gray of overcast or the black of night made it seem ominous before. In the daylight it was just a total delight.

"It's not what it seems," said the blue Crony.

"What do you mean?"

This intruder was becoming bothersome. If the king didn't send him, why was he wasting his time with him.

"Isn't something missing?"

"Like what?"

"Like rain."

"I like it better this way."

"It only seems better."

"What's wrong with it?"

"Tell me, what do you do when it's raining?"

"I go inside out of the rain."

"Why?"

"So I don't get wet." This is getting stupid, Jimmy thought. What does he take me for, a child?

"Listen, friend," the Crony said. "The rain makes you go inside so that you won't get struck by lightning."

"That's ridiculous!"

"Believe me. I wouldn't put you on."

"Well, I'm not putting you on either when I tell you to take off. I'm going in there. It looks like fun to me."

"Sometimes things that seem bad, like rain, are good, and things that seem good are bad. That's what I'm your Crony for. So, before you go in there, let me give you a word of advice,

> Don't touch a Krank.
> Don't touch a Krank.
> Let me be perfectly frank.
> Don't touch a Krank.

"What is that supposed to mean?" Jimmy was annoyed but strangely intrigued by the creature.

"Mark my words well, my friend," he said and disappeared into the blue.

Suddenly, lightning flashed all around him so that he couldn't see. When it stopped he saw young people like himself all around him. They were everywhere, all young, all like himself. The sight of all of them made him feel comfortable.

One of them came up to Jimmy. "Welcome," she said. "It's good to see you here. We love to have company. We want people to feel warm and comfortable here."

Jimmy noticed that a sort of warm glow came out of her like a soft white light bulb.

"The way it looks just before it bursts out of existence like a flash-bulb!" The voice was that of the Crony, but there was no one there. He looked at the girl again and thought of a soft summer evening, when the warm moist air is filled with the smell of blossoms.

"Like just before it rains and flashes lightning!"

"Stop that!" Jimmy shouted.

"Stop what?" she asked. "We would just like you to be one with us."

"Who's us?"

"The people who live here."

Suddenly, there were more of them all around him. "Hello," "Welcome," they said extending their hands in greeting. They all seemed so warm and loving.

"Thank you," Jimmy said. "You're all so wonderful. Who are you?"

"We're called Kranks and we want to be one with you," the girl said. "Come and join us."

"Why not?" Jimmy said reaching out to take one of them by the hand. As his hand approached hers he felt warmth coming out of it. The closer their hands got the hotter it became.

> Don't touch a Krank.
> Don't touch a Krank.
> Let me be perfectly frank.
> Don't touch a Krank.

"Why not?" she said.

The instant before their hands met Jimmy's hand turned blue. When he touched her he felt warmth surge through his body. It was a wonderful, good feeling. Then the warmth accelerated and it became uncomfortably hot. He tried to withdraw his hand but he couldn't. The hot became electric like summer lightning. He was caught as if he were holding a live electric wire and not able to let go. They were welding together. Jimmy screamed out in terror.

Instantly, the pain was gone. His blue hand was still stretched out. They hadn't touched yet. Jimmy realized that he was given a flash of what would happen. He quickly withdrew his hand and it turned back to its normal color. For a brief moment he realized that he had put on the blue Crony.

He was standing alone in a big hall. There was a big celebration going on. The tables were filled with food and partying people were laughing everywhere. The blue Crony was standing next to him.

> Don't choose a Schmooze.
> Don't choose a Schmooze.
> If you don't want to lose.
> Don't choose a Schmooze.

"What's with the rhymes? Will you get serious, old man?"

"I am serious," said the Crony. "Will you get serious?"

"This is not a time for serious. This is party time. So, get lost, will you?"

Jimmy walked around from table to table looking at the people. They all seemed perfectly normal. And they were all overwhelmingly happy.

"That's for me!" Jimmy thought. "That old blue Crony is giving me the spooks. This is what I've been waiting for."

"Don't choose a Schmooze!"

Just to make sure, Jimmy walked around again watching all the partyers. They were eating and drinking and laughing hysterically. What more could he want? Just as he was ready to jump into this scene his eyes turned blue.

They were still laughing hysterically. Putting on blue Crony hadn't changed a thing. The warning was mistaken. He approached a table of revelers. When he got really close is when he saw it. The hysterical laughter was actually hysterical crying! They were crying, not laughing. From a distance it seemed like the same thing. It sounded like the same thing. Jimmy caught it just in time. Had he jumped in, he might not have been able to jump out again. He heaved a sigh of relief as his eyes turned back to normal again.

This time he called the Crony.

"What is all this about?" he asked.

"This is a strange land. Here, nothing is for certain yet. Things aren't always what they seem either. That's why I'm here to help you. I'm your Crony."

"Did King Shoddy send you."

"Heavens no! Much of what you see here is his doing. And there is still more. Not everything is bad. As a matter of fact, there is much you can enjoy here. All you need is a little bit of help from your Crony."

"Like what else should I know?"

"Try this:

> Don't hug a Slug.
> Don't hug a Slug.
> They're the worst kind of a bug.
> Don't hug a Slug."

"I don't even know what a Slug is!" Jimmy said. He was quickly losing patience with all this. He liked to jump into things on his own without any advice from anyone.

"That's a Slug!" The Crony pointed to a dreamy-eyed character who just suddenly appeared. "And that's a Slug!" He pointed to another dreamy-eyed character. "And there! And there!" They were all around and they looked like marvellous, pleasant people. They smiled and giggled. They seemed to float rather than walk. And they were exceptionally pleasant and jovial. They walked around embracing each other, inviting others to join them.

Jimmy watched them for hours. There was absolutely nothing awry here. The Crony was making him too hesitant. He was spoiling all his fun. It was about time for him to get into this place. To get into something. Anything. He decided to throw all foolish caution to the wind and hug a Slug.

Just then the true, blue Crony turned the sky to dark blue. It became so dark it was almost night.

"You're not going to stop me this time," Jimmy yelled. "I'm going to hug a Slug even if it's pitch dark outside."

"The dark is not meant to stop you," he said, "but to show you what they're like at night."

"I don't care what they're like at night," Jimmy shouted. "I want to hug a Slug!"

Just then all the Slugs that were hugging began scratching. Wherever one touched another the Slug began to itch uncontrollably. Everywhere they touched one another they got welts like mosquito bites. Everyone now was scratching all over.

"Mosquitoes come out at dusk," Jimmy thought.

"They're the worst kind of a bug," the Crony reminded him.

"I give up," Jimmy said. "I want to go back."

"I'm afraid there's no more going back," the Crony said.

"Then I want to get out of here!"

"Why?"

"Because everything goes wrong here and I haven't done anything yet."

"No, not everything. I tell you this place isn't half bad. There a lot of wonderful things here. There are happy things and crazy times and wonderful memories."

"Where? Where will I find them? How will I find them?"

"All you need is a true blue Crony to help you. Listen, my friend..."

"Oh, no!" Jimmy sighed. "I feel another rhyme coming on."

> "Be happy and free.
> Do biscuits and tea.

But stay close behind me.
And become all that you can be."

The blue Crony took Jimmy by the hand and started leading him through the wonderful Strange Land of Yet.

But this story doesn't have an ending because they haven't gone through all of this strange land...yet!

~ Moral ~

Adolescence is the Strange Land of Yet
where love can be an unwanted and cranky commitment,
alcohol leave you laughing on the outside
but crying on the inside
and drugs in torturous pain.
All teenagers need a true blue crony
to help them get through it.

 Advice

Until you've cleaned a baby's behind
at least a thousand times
you shouldn't tell a mother
how to raise children.

~ 32 ~

The Antique Box

IT WAS CHRISTMAS. The presents were numerous and extravagant. All except one. It was a box. An old one, unwrapped and unadorned. You could say antique, only that might imply something it obviously was not — valuable. Ancient and eccentric Aunt Martha gave it to her, mumbling something about its being around for generations. She accepted it graciously and placed it alongside the latest designer dress, a jewel-studded watch, and the Waterford decanter set. It looked like a sow's ear lying there.

She put it away afterward, on the top shelf of the hallway closet.

It gathered dust there for some three or four years until she got caught unawares by her best friend's husband's birthday. "He likes old things," she said to her husband, as he brought the box down from its resting place. "We'll tell him its an antique we got for him at an auction."

Her friend's husband was pleased and curious about it. "Is there anything in it?" he asked.

"You got it like we got it," she laughed a bit apprehensively. "As is!"

It suddenly dawned on her that she had never thought to look inside. For just a fleeting moment she felt a pang of remorse. What if there were something really valuable inside and she was giving it away.

She would never forgive herself. Neither would her husband. She thought of her now deceased eccentric aunt and seriously doubted it.

"That's what makes the gift so special," she said, winking at her husband. "It could be a treasure or it could be a pig in a poke."

There was a moment's breathlessness as he undid the fastener and opened the box. He said nothing. The others could see nothing. The suspense was unbearable.

"Well!" they all said in unison.

A grin broke across his face. He reached inside the box and took out an old pair of granny glasses. Everyone roared with delight as he forced them on his large face.

"I guess I got the pig," he bellowed.

There were some other things inside. Old things, but nothing really valuable. He rummaged through them, displaying them to the hearty laughs of everyone at the party.

~

She sighed in relief. Her gift had been the hit of the party.

The next day he took a few things that he liked from the box, an old daguerreotype, a pocket watch and chain, and a tarnished hand mirror. He then stored the box in the attic.

Two years later when his son was on semester break from college he discovered the box.

"Hey, Dad. I need something like this to put my stuff in at school and lock it. My roommates are always taking my things. Mind if I take it?"

"Go right ahead, son."

"What do you want me to do with the stuff that's inside?"

"I took all that I wanted from there. If you don't want anything else, dump it."

That's what he did and carted it off to college. It got more use with him than it had had for years. He kept his watches, rings, and other valuables locked up in it.

When graduation approached and he was getting ready to clean out and clear out, he eventually got to the antique box. He emptied it of all his possessions and was going to discard it. But somehow it had developed a kind of sentimental value over these past three and a half years. It just didn't feel right to throw it away. So he decided to clean it up instead and put his things back into it.

While he was cleaning the inside he tried to remove some paper clips that had gotten lodged between the bottom and sides of the box. He flipped the box upside down and tapped against the bottom. It took several hard raps before he heard a thump. Something had fallen onto the table. When he lifted the box he saw that it had a false bottom. There was an old yellowed paper wrapped around a few tarnished coins.

Carefully, he unfolded the paper. It was a letter. From General George Washington. It was to some poor family that had helped him and his troops at Valley Forge. The coins were to help the family. They were the first ones minted by the new government of the United States of America.

~ Moral ~

*Look carefully before you discard
what may seem to be old and worthless.*

~ 33 ~

The Bishop's Pearl

ONCE UPON A TIME in the days when bishops ruled over cities and cardinals over countries, a great but unwise cardinal came to preside at the baptism of his brother's son. During the festivities that followed everyone waited anxiously to see what wondrous gift the wealthy cardinal would give his nephew.

Vested in an ermine cape and a crimson robe, more dazzling than any peacock in full array, the cardinal rose from his place at the head of the banquet table and waited peevishly for the assembly to settle down.

"My gift to my nephew on this day of his christening," he paused to make sure that his announcement had everyone's full attention, "is the promise that when he has grown to manhood, I will make him bishop over a great city."

The cardinal fully expected to hear excited oohs and aahs burst forth from the guests. Instead they treated his announcement in the manner it deserved — as a meaningless diversion. Only his brother seemed pleased. Why should the others be excited? After all, it was something they had all expected anyway. This was a paltry gift indeed, coming from one so rich and powerful. If he wanted to impress the crowd, he would have to do better than a bishopric.

But since the cardinal was not a generous man he had nothing else in mind. A bishopric should have been enough to please any man, and it most certainly pleased the boy's father. Still, the assembly made absolutely nothing of it. Instead, they simply continued bantering and gossiping. It would take something much bigger than that to get their attention again.

The cardinal was infuriated and embarrassed. He was a man of monumental pride, and even though he was stingy with his benefices he knew that he would now have to do something uncharacteristically extravagant to redeem his honor.

It so happened that on his way to the christening he had stayed overnight at a certain nobleman's castle. Wanting to curry favor with the cardinal, the man offered him a magnificent pearl in exchange for a title and lands. The pearl was bigger and better than any the cardinal himself had or ever saw. It was almost the size of a baby's fist. At once the greedy cardinal knew that he had to have it, so he agreed to the deal. Now as he stood shame-faced before the assembly, he realized that only the pearl could help him save face. He unfastened the purse attached to his belt and held it aloft for everyone to see. Once he had everyone's attention again, he opened the purse and extracted the pearl. It had the desired effect. Everyone oohed and aahed appropriately. While this pleased the cardinal, it came at the price of a broken heart. He would much rather have kept the pearl for himself.

The cardinal's brother took the priceless pearl and put it into his son's hand. The child could barely grasp it. As the guests laughed delightedly an old hermit who had come in from the woods for the great event came forward. He looked at the baby clutching the pearl in its tiny hand and then at the cardinal.

"What have you done to this child?" he screamed, pointing a bony finger at the fat prelate. "Blessed are the poor, said the Lord. Would you corrupt this infant on the very day of his baptism with mammon?"

Never one to be outdone by prince or even pope, for his quick wit had brought him this far, the cardinal quickly countered the old man:

"I have given my nephew the pearl of great price, which the Lord says a man should sell everything he has in order to purchase."

The hermit stared the cardinal in the eye for a long time, which made the great prince of the church more than a little nervous. "We shall see if it is manna or mammon that you have given this child." Turning to the infant in the crib, he said, "One day child, your eyes will tell the tale." Having said that, he stormed out of the banquet hall.

Some people said that the hermit had cursed the child. Others argued that holy men do not curse and that it was the gift that was a curse. So it went. The child was cursed. The pearl was cursed. The cardinal was cursed. The day was cursed. In any event everyone agreed that something was cursed that fateful day.

The child grew to manhood, and as the cardinal promised he was consecrated a bishop. Several times he was approached by his uncle with offers for the pearl, but the youth had proved as greedy and resourceful as the old man in refusing him. This was why the great prelate refused to ordain him himself but got some feeble and dissolute bishop instead to do the job.

Now it must be said that the young bishop like his uncle the cardinal was a clever and ambitious man if not a holy one. Bishops are not holy just because they are bishops, any more than Christians are holy because they are baptized. There were two things in his life that he guarded jealously — his position and the pearl. He allowed no one in his city to overshadow him, and the pearl he had fashioned into a ring, which he made all who came to see him genuflect and kiss. The former gave him great pleasure. But the latter disturbed him because he saw the lust with which everyone stared at his priceless gem. Still there was no sense in owning a beautiful jewel if he could not show it off or in being a bishop if he could not flaunt it. So he kept a careful eye out for anyone who carefully eyed either of his prizes. The hermit's words had proven prophetic.

One day a simple green grocer's son while playing in the woods chanced upon the old hermit's hut. In return for helping him gather firewood, the hermit gave the boy a pretty colored stone. "It is not valuable," he said, "but always remember that value is in the eye of the beholder." Upon returning to the city the boy discovered that all his young friends wanted the pretty stone for themselves. The way many of them eyed it, he knew that given the chance they would steal it away from him. He liked the stone and he liked his friends, so rather than hide it or flaunt it or have it stolen he let whoever wanted it borrow it. This pleased everyone and made him very popular.

For some strange reason the attraction for the stone continued even as he grew into manhood. Some said that the holy hermit had cast a spell on it. Others argued that witches and not hermits cast spells. So it went. The stone was blessed. The grocer's son was blessed. The people were blessed because he continued to let everyone who wanted it borrow it. This made him very popular and the bishop very jealous.

As months passed into years, the young man's pretty colored stone became a greater attraction than the bishop's fabled pearl. The bishop had to do something. The young man would gladly have let him borrow the stone as he did with everyone else, but the prelate was much too proud to ask. Besides, bishops don't borrow, they possess. At least, that's what this bishop believed. Since he couldn't bear being humbled by anyone, let alone a peasant, he decided that he would have to get rid of the green grocer's son.

On the guise of making him a special envoy, the bishop sent him off to a leper colony. The move was both expedient and ingenious. In one stroke he rid himself of the irksome young man and his annoying popularity, for who would dare risk following him to such a dreaded place? He would soon be forgotten. With the green grocer's son and the colored stone affair successfully dealt with, the bishop got back down to business.

However, it was not to be. The bishop could not get the confounded stone out of his mind. Before long, it became an obsession.

He thought about having one of his minions steal it, but decided against it because he could never show it to anyone, and what good is a precious stone if you can't show it off? That's when he resolved to find another like it. After all, one should not be hard to come by; it was nothing more than a common stone.

The minute others knew of his intentions, there was no lack of ambitious young men bringing him colored stones. At first, he was extremely pleased. He even rewarded them with offices within his household. Still others came bearing gifts, and more benefices were doled out.

Before long, however, the proud prelate became dismayed. His appetite simply became more insatiable. He was like someone who cannot stop eating at a banquet even though his stomach is full. Over the years he had accumulated chests and chests of pretty colored stones. Instead of pleasing him, the opposite was true. He realized better than most that the more there is of something the less valuable it becomes. People had even begun paying off their debts to him in colored stones, making him appear the fool. In addition to this, not all his stones put together gave him an iota of the popularity the one stone had given the grocer's son. He was convinced that he had indeed been cursed by the old hermit.

Desperate to remove the weight of this burden from his life, the bishop went off on retreat to a mountain sanctuary. Away from the passions engendered by his position, he began to feel deep remorse over all that he had done. He needed to free his conscience by confessing. His pride would suffer no damage here in this remote place where no one knew him.

In the quiet darkness and anonymity of a backwater village confessional, the bishop poured out his soul to the priest just as countless peasants had, for in the secrecy of the confessional all people are truly equal. The wise priest listened in grave silence and offered no remonstrations or advice. As penance he said to the prelate, "You must loan your pearl to all who come asking."

The bishop was aghast. Loan out his precious pearl to anyone and everyone? Was the priest mad? He might never get it back. He criticized the confessor for such a strict penance and ordered him to commute it. The priest refused, for in the administration of the sacrament a lowly priest stands equal even to the pope. The bishop stormed out of the little church and returned to his diocese in great consternation. Everyone saw his turmoil, but even those closest to him were at a loss over how to console him. The bishop stormed and raged about his castle for weeks.

Then one day the green grocer's son came calling. The bishop barely recognized him he had so aged during his work among the lepers. He was indeed a pathetic sight in his wretched and smelly clothes. The bishop sneered as he remembered that he had once been jealous of this pitiful creature.

"What is it you want?" he asked, trying to guard his nose against the man's foul smell.

"Your Excellency," he said, "we have nothing left in our colony to provide for even the most basic needs of food and drink. If I do not return with help, we will all surely die."

"What is it to me?" the bishop exclaimed, savoring his revenge. "I have a city to run and my expenses are monumental. Everything here comes at a price. The farmers and merchants give me nothing. What will you give me to offer them in exchange?"

The poor man reached into his pocket and took out the colored stone. "This is all I have," he said.

There it was. That awful, wretched stone that had caused him so many years of anguish and turmoil. Now it was his for the taking, only he no longer wanted it. He saw how worthless it truly was and laughed.

"I'll tell you what," he said. Remembering his still undone penance, he removed the pearl ring from his finger and held it out to him. "Keep your useless stone. You may take mine."

The bishop was visibly annoyed when the poor man didn't fall all over himself with gratitude. True, he was grateful, but unaccountably reserved. It was almost as if he half expected what the bishop said next. "For only a week. If you do not return it within a week I will have you severely punished, if not executed."

The bishop fully expected the man to resent being baited, but instead his face beamed as he replied, "A week is more than enough."

Exactly a week to the day and hour, the poor grocer's son returned with the ring. He also had a full cartload of supplies for his precious lepers.

"How did you do this?" the bishop asked.

"I did with the bishop's pearl what I once did with the colored stone I was given as a boy. I showed it around to everyone. As a holy hermit once told me, value is in the eye of the beholder. I knew that many people would come forward who wanted the pearl. When they did I told them that I would gladly let them borrow it but only for a limited time, since I only had it for a limited time."

"So then," said the bishop triumphantly, "you were indeed a wise and prudent servant. You charged them for the rental of the stone. Well done!" The bishop was honest enough to appreciate good industry wherever he encountered it.

"Not at all!" the man replied. "I charged them nothing. It was theirs free for whatever time it was available to them."

"Then how did you come by all the goods in your cart?"

"A countess used the ring during a party and gave me all the left-over food. A duke used it to impress a jealous rival and rewarded me with bread and game. A tavern keeper used it to show his customers, which gave him added business. He gave me wine and ale for the use of the ring. So it continued throughout the week. Had I rented out your ring, precious few people would have been able to afford it and I would have received not nearly enough to take back with me. Now I have a full cartload and the people's gratitude."

The bishop marveled at his tale. "Where did you learn this wisdom?"

"From an old hermit who learned it from his master who taught him that it is more blessed to give than to receive."

The green grocer's son left with a light heart and a heavy cart, which was made even heavier by the bishop's gratitude for what he learned.

It happened afterward that the bishop gladly fulfilled his long overdue penance by loaning out his precious pearl to any and all who came asking for it. In return he received gifts beyond his wildest dreams and the gratitude of a people who prospered because of his generosity and good example.

Finally, he returned to the tiny chapel in the poor mountain village to thank the confessor for the penance that had changed his life. The dark of the confessional was made bright by the once proud prelate's humble gratitude. As he exited the Angelus bell rang, summoning the peasants for evening prayer. One by one they filed past the prelate, stopping briefly to genuflect and kiss his ring. As they did he noticed the sores on their faces and hands. They were lepers. He had stumbled upon a leper colony. He looked back into the tiny church. He smiled knowingly and then laughed when he saw that the priest who came out of the confessional to lead his people in prayer was none other than the green grocer's son.

~ Moral ~

Nothing is more valuable than a generous heart.

 *The Bishop*

A bishop is called a "prelate."
How can one be "pre-late,"
unless it means that he is late before his time?

~ *34* ~

Brothers

O<small>NE DAY</small> a father gave his two sons each a basket and sent them into the world with this advice: "The purpose of life is to become wealthy. Go out and make your fortune." On the way the one brother found some money, and put it into his basket. Once he had money he learned very quickly about all the wonderful things money could do and buy. Thus, he devoted his life to doing whatever he could to find money, get money and make money. His brother on the other hand went about putting into his basket just a little bit of this and maybe some of that.

In the end the one brother became an extremely rich man while the other brother had . . . only money.

 Commandments

God has ten commandments.
Money has a million.

35

Two Philosophers

ONE DAWN as the sun rose above the mountains, one philosopher said to the other, "Let's go on a journey to Olympus."

"What do you mean?" asked the other philosopher.

"I mean let's take a delightful trip to the mountain."

"How can you 'take' something which is not takeable?" said the second philosopher. "You can take a coat or a sweater or even a walking stick, but how can you take something that is not material? How can you take something that is immaterial and therefore not really there?"

"Then instead of 'take,'" said the first philosopher, "let me say 'make.' Let's make a journey and go to Olympus."

"That's no better," said the second philosopher. "How does one make a journey? With wood? With bricks and mortar? To make something or anything presupposes materiality. There is no materiality there."

"There is by way of analogy," the first philosopher retorted. "Materiality by way of analogy."

"What do you mean by analogy?"

"I mean two things that are somewhat the same yet totally different."

"That's a contradiction in terms."

"That depends on whose terms. Are we speaking classical philosophy or modern existentialist?"

"Classical."

"Classical philosophy is dated and irrelevant."

"Modern existential philosophy is indecisive and irresponsible."

"Says you."

"Say you."

"What do you mean?"

"The proper grammar is 'say you,' not 'says you.'"

" 'Says you' is allowed under certain circumstances."

"What circumstances?"

"It depends on whether one chooses to use classical grammar or modern idiomatic, living grammar."

"Idiomatic is idiotic."

"Idiotic if one holds to dead forms like some hold to dead languages. Does the language form the people or do the people form the language?"

"That's a Sophist trap like 'Have you stopped beating your wife?'" screamed the second philosopher. "I deny the basic supposition."

"To deny my basic supposition is an affront to my intelligence," shouted the first philosopher.

"What intelligence?" snorted the second philosopher.

At this point the first philosopher struck the second philosopher in the nose. The second philosopher replied that every force in nature is balanced by an equal counterforce and hit him in the head. A classical existential battle ensued — which all goes to prove the perennial truth that splitting hairs often ends up in splitting heads.

In the end the journey or trip to Olympus was never taken or made or even begun.

36

The Burden:
A Tale of the Christ

ONCE THERE WAS a great and powerful king whose kingdom stretched farther and wider than that of any other king and whose authority was total and absolute.

One day a young man committed a serious offense against the king. The opinion of all his advisors was unanimous. For one so lowly to offend against one so mighty the only just sentence possible was death. So it would have been decreed had it not been for the king's son. He was the young man's friend, so he pleaded before the king for leniency and mercy.

"This cannot be," a royal counselor objected. "If such an offense against your august personage were to go unpunished, it would be allowing a breach against the order of the realm. To allow one is to allow others. Eventually there will be chaos in the kingdom and everyone would suffer. For the kingdom to survive justice must prevail."

"It is so," the others agreed. "The sentence must be death."

"Consider if you will that the king's personage is so august," pleaded the son, "that any offense no matter how small would have to be punished by death. Eventually, there would be no chaos in the kingdom as there would be no kingdom."

Thus the debate raged on, the royal advisors demanding justice, the king's son calling for mercy.

At last, the king decided. "The offender must pay a price for his offense. A heavy price. Therefore, I decree that he be made to carry a heavy burden up Temple Mountain. If he survives the ordeal, he shall live."

The royal advisors stormed out of the council chambers in protest against the king's judgment. Had the chaos begun?

Knowing that the burden his friend would carry must bear the weight of death and that he would not be strong enough for the task, the king's son again intervened. "Royal blood has been offended so only royal blood can pay the price. The decree will be fulfilled and justice satisfied, but I will carry the load," he said.

So the king's son shouldered the heavy burden and began the arduous trek up the steep mountain. In his wake followed the young offender.

The task was terrible indeed, for the higher the prince climbed the heavier the load became. He stumbled numerous times along the way, but he somehow always managed to rise and continue on again. When he finally came within sight of the summit, however, he collapsed.

"For there to be peace in the kingdom, the price must be paid," the prince gasped to his friend. The young man knew what he must do. Weak as he was, the prince's friend lifted the burden onto his own shoulders and struggled desperately with it all the way to the top.

The entire kingdom now stretched out before them. With a final effort the king's son reached down and lifted the load high above his head for the whole world to see.

"It is done," he said and died.

"Justice is satisfied," said the king, who then with his awesome power over life and death called his son back to life.

"Not yet," said his son come to life again.

"How so?" asked the king.

"Royal blood was helped along the way. My friend assisted me in my agony. Therefore, justice demands that he receive an equal reward."

"So be it!" decreed the king.

So the prince and the offender lived happily ever after. And so also may we.

 Bible

The Bible is inspired but not everything in it is inspiring.

 Footprints

Life is the footprint of God.
Wherever you see life
you know that God walked there.

~ 37 ~

The Sacred Coin

ON THE SIXTH DAY God created Father Adam and Mother Eve.
On the seventh day as God was resting, they asked Him if He would give them something special to commemorate their birthday. So God reached into His treasure chest and took out a sacred coin. Written on it was the word "LOVE."

On the eighth day Father Adam and Mother Eve sinned. As they left the Garden of Eden they asked God for an assurance that He would not abandon them.

"You have the coin," He told them.

"But, the coin says LOVE," they answered. "We have lost love. How ever will we find it again?"

"Turn it over," God said.

On the other side of the coin was written the word "FORGIVENESS."

During the thousands of years of this ninth day of the world humanity has had to learn that there is no love without forgiveness and no forgiveness without love. They are the two sides of the same coin.

~ 38 ~

Colors

ONCE UPON A TIME there was a great and loving king who ruled over a vast and mighty kingdom. The strange thing about his kingdom was that all the people everywhere wore the same clothes, ate the same food, drank the same drink, and did the same work. And everything was gray. Their clothes were gray. Their food was gray. Their drink was gray. Even their work was gray. There were no colors.

Then one day as the sun was setting a strange bird, as if from a myth, flew out of the west into the kingdom. It came to an obscure village and deposited a yellow egg. Never had the people seen such a remarkably beautiful thing. They marveled at its sun-like brilliance. How did the egg get its magnificent color? Curiosity eventually drove them to break open the egg to discover its secret. They found that it contained a yellow powder. To their added delight they discovered that whatever they sprinkled the powder on also turned yellow. In no time at all they had sprinkled the powder on almost everything in the village.

The next evening at sunset the bird emerged again and flew into a different village and deposited another egg. Only this time the egg was blue. Before long everyone and everything in this village had turned blue.

So it continued for seven straight evenings. Each time the bird deposited an egg of a different colored. Each village prided itself on its different color.

When news of the strange happenings eventually reached the king, he called together his wisest counselors to explain this odd phenomenon. They searched the ancient manuscripts but could find no such incident ever having occurred before in the annals of the kingdom. However, they did uncover information that could seriously affect the future, if not the very life of the kingdom.

"We've discovered that many long generations ago, our kingdom was once ruled by a mighty philosopher king. At that time, the kingdom was plagued with endless internal conflicts. Cities battled against cities and villages against villages. The king reasoned that all such contentions resulted from the differences that existed among the peoples. Since he wanted peace he simply ruled out differences. Everything must be the same. Thus, there would be no cause for dissension. It was he who decreed that everyone and everything must be gray. So it has been for a thousand years."

Immediately, the king called in twelve of his finest archers and ordered them to shoot the bird that laid the colored eggs. At sunset when the bird flew out of the west the archers did as the king commanded. They shot the great winged creature. Each of their arrows flew true and struck its mark. Incredibly, however, the missiles passed through the bird without so much as injuring it. It simply continued on its journey.

If the bird could not be stopped, the king decreed, then the people must be stopped. They must not use its eggs to change the color of things. They must all go back to gray.

However, the decree was ignored. So the king sent his army to force his subjects to comply. Instead, they rebelled. For many long months a battle raged. Meanwhile, the bird continued to fly and lay its eggs, causing the fighting to spread to still other villages and get worse.

"There will be no kingdom left if the war continues," the royal counselors advised the king.

"But the past has shown us that the same will happen if we allow there to be differences among the people," the king retorted. "Then in either event the kingdom will perish," sighed the king.

The stalemate continued as the war raged on.

Then one day, the great bird flew into the very palace of the king and deposited seven beautifully colored eggs there. In a fit of frenzy, or by an act of divine mercy, the outraged king hurled the seven eggs in all directions. They burst into an array of colors. The beauty of it all so amazed the king that in a moment of inspiration he knew exactly what to do.

The next day the king decreed that *all* the people should have *all* the colors. Thus the wars ceased and peace returned to the land.

From that day on since all the people had all the colors there were no more contentions, so they all lived happily ever after.

 Sunbeams

If you eat enough sunbeams,
you will turn into sunlight.

~ 39 ~

The Dam

AT THE TOP OF A MOUNTAIN there was a great crater lake. In the valley below the people were in serious need of water. They realized that they couldn't simply dig a channel and allow the water to spill out, because that would just flood the valley. What they needed was a dam. So they got an engineer to plan and help them build a dam.

The engineer carefully studied the lay of the land, the qualities of the rock and the soil, the future direction of the water flow, the amount of pressure that would or could be exerted, and a thousand and one other things important to the planning of a dam.

Then construction began. It continued for many long and tedious months until, at long last, the project was finished. They had truly built a great and glorious dam.

When the dam gates were ceremoniously opened to release the water to the waiting valley below, nothing came out. They had used up all the water in the lake to build the dam.

~ Moral ~

You can't give what you no longer have.

Three Men in a Desert

THE KINGDOM OF GOD is like three men wandering in a desert. One of them chanced upon a water hole. He took a quick drink and quickly covered it over so that no one else would find it.

The second man came upon a verdant valley that stretched for miles and miles. Only he cultivated just a tiny little plot that was barely enough for him to get by on.

The third discovered a mountain cave filled with treasure. He carried all of it off with him and lived prosperously and well.

 Friendship

When friendship says, "Scratch my back,"
love will always find a way.

 Friends and Enemies

Don't get mad at your friends,
or the only ones left will be your enemies.

The Diamond

A NOVICE came before his master and asked what he must do before he could become a full wizard like his master.

"It is not so much what you must do," the sage replied, "as what you must learn."

"What must I learn, then?" the youth asked, impatient to take his place alongside the wise man.

The wizard lay on the table before him a number of precious stones: a ruby red as crimson blood, an emerald green as valley grass after a rainfall, a sapphire more blue than the sea and the sky, an onyx blacker than coal, a topaz gold as the sun, and an uncut diamond.

The wizard put the uncut diamond in a small sack and drew the drawstrings together. He gave it to the boy saying, "When you can tell me why this diamond is more valuable than all the other stones combined you will be ready to take your place beside me. For now, you must learn."

So the wizard sent the youth off to school. The boy saw no real value in this because he wanted to be a wizard, and nothing they taught there was anything like his master's magic. Mathematics was pure frustration. Time and again its perplexities so angered him, its intricacies so confounded him that it made his blood boil and his face turn crimson. The study of literature, however, placated him.

He would seek solace there and become placid as the sea and the sky. Sports showed him that there were others more gifted and agile than he so he had to learn to deal with his jealousy and envy. During this time he also found friendship and love, which warmed his heart and made him glow like the sun. Through the years he endured and learned.

When, at last, his school days were finished, he went back to the wizard.

"What have you learned my son?" he asked, looking lovingly at the young man through eyes that sparkled like diamonds.

"I have learned, great master, that an uncut diamond has no value. It is less precious than all the other stones individually or together."

"And why is that so?" the master asked.

"Because uncut, it reflects no light. Only when it is cut does it contain the red of the ruby, the green of the emerald, the blue of the sapphire, and the gold of the topaz. That is why it is more valuable than all the other stones, which can boast of only one color."

"This you learned *in* school?" the wizard continued.

"This I learned while *at* school," he said smiling. "Each experience, each frustration, every accomplishment cut into the diamond of my life."

The young man took the still unopened sack and handed it back to the master. The wizard opened it to reveal a beautifully chiseled precious stone.

"This one I shall call Alma Mater," he said, as the young man came forward to take his place beside him.

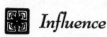 *Influence*

I can affect the entire universe
by touching my own little corner of the world.

42

The Legend of the Christ Dove

THERE IS AN ANCIENT LEGEND found in one form or another among all the peoples of the earth that once upon a time the gates of heaven were always open wide so that both angels and people could pass back and forth through them as freely as they wished. Then, when Adam and Eve sinned against God and creation, the gates were closed tight, nevermore to remain open.

Countless thousands of years passed, but only once did the gates of heaven open and then, only for a moment, when the son of God left heaven to come to earth. On the eighth day after he was born, his mother took the child to the Temple to pay the price for the child's redemption — two turtle doves for those who are poor. When the priest went to offer them in sacrifice, one of them escaped and flew off. But the bird could find no place on earth to rest, the reason being that the one dove had paid the price for the humanity of Christ and there is no price than can equal his divinity. So the bird had nowhere to go except heaven. However, when it got there the gates were closed.

Standing before the gates the turtle dove began to sing its dear, sweet, melodious song. So uncommonly wonderful was its hymn that the Father Himself came to open the gates thinking that His son had returned. When He saw just the dove standing there, He sent it back to earth to bring back His son.

"When you return and sing your sweet song I will open the gates of heaven again so that you may enter."

When the dove returned to earth, the child was gone from Jerusalem and was nowhere to be found in all the Holy Land. Weary from its travels the dove needed a place to rest. Since the bird could not light on earth nor enter heaven it flew to the only place where innocence exists between heaven and earth — the heart of a child. It cradled itself there until it could gather enough strength to continue its search.

It is said that the child immediately took on the nature of the dove, sweet and gentle and kind. Then as the dove-child grew, the bird continued to gather strength until it was strong enough to leave and continue its search for the Christ child.

But before it did, it carried the soul of its host to the gates of heaven and sang its sweet, plaintive song. On hearing the Christ Dove the Father opened the gates of heaven and allowed the soul to pass through.

Since then the Christ Dove continually journeys back and forth between heaven and earth, taking up residence in the hearts of the innocent until the day it can find the Christ Child once again.

~ 43 ~

Dreamweaver

ONCE UPON A TIME there was a little girl who had a dream. It was a wonderful and happy dream that made her feel good all over. It was the kind of dream you want to hold on to for as long as you possibly can. But even as she thought about it, it began to slip away until she couldn't remember it at all anymore.

When she told her mother, her mother said that a dream is like the wind. You don't know where it comes from. You feel it for just a short time, and it goes off to you don't know where.

"But how can you capture a dream?" the little girl asked.

"Tell it to someone," the mother replied.

So the next time the girl had a dream she ran off to tell her friends about it. She did so again and again with every dream. But when she wanted to talk to her friends about her dreams, she discovered that they all had so many dreams of their own and had heard about so many others that they couldn't remember hers anymore.

"What do I now?" she asked her mother.

"Tell them to a special friend," she said.

So she found a special friend and told him about her dreams every time she had one. And he told her his. Whenever they were together they shared all their dreams. Soon there were so many dreams he couldn't remember all hers, nor she his.

"What now?" she asked her mother.

"Go to the dreamweaver," she said.

Now the dreamweaver was a truly remarkable man. He could weave the blue of dreams into sapphires, the greens into emeralds, reds into rubies, and yellows into golden sunsets. Together she and her special friend went to the dreamweaver, and he wove each of their dreams into a brilliant tapestry.

Yet, in time, even this was not enough. They had accumulated so many marvelous tapestries that the dreams somehow got lost in the very beauty of his works.

"Where do we go from here?" she asked the dreamweaver.

So he wove the two of them together, so that every dream of hers was his and every dream of his was hers. This itself was like a dream, a wonderful and happy dream that made them feel good all over. It was the kind of dream that made them want to hold on to it for as long as they possibly could. But they didn't want this dream to pass like all the others. Nor did they want to admire it for its own sake like the tapestry. They wanted this dream *to live*.

"What now?" they asked the dreamweaver.

"Only God can make a dream live and last," he said. "Go to God."

So they went to God, knowing that God alone gives life to all things.

"Give this dream life," they asked. God granted their request. So the dream became flesh and dwelt among them.

The Fish

ONCE UPON A TIME there was a fish who lived in a stagnant pool. Breathing was so difficult there that it was fast becoming a desperate situation. He decided to call his friends together and brave the unknown to find more livable waters.

Their journey was difficult and precarious, but in the end they were successful when they chanced upon a gently flowing babbling brook.

"This is where we must make our new home," said the fish. "And to make sure that we do not lose what we have found," he continued, "we must safeguard it."

Together they scoured around until they found enough materials and debris to make a carefully closed in compound for themselves.

"What we have is safe now!" they cried out in exaltation.

Unfortunately, they had boxed themselves in far too well, so that in the end they all died from lack of oxygen.

~ Moral ~

What is not shared is lost.

~ 45 ~

The Flower Lady

ONE EVENING a workman was wearily plodding his way home when he stopped to rest by the side of the road. A woman came by the place hauling a cart filled with flowers. The smell of her blossoms so perfumed the air with sweetness that just the smell of them seemed to take away the weariness in his bones and lighten his spirits. He had never experienced such wonder from the many blooms of his own garden.

"How much must I pay or what must I do to have some of your wonderful flowers?" he asked the woman.

"Good, sir. Take what you wish," she replied.

"What return must I make for them?" he questioned again.

"Your gratitude is enough," she said.

The man filled his arms with blossoms and hastened home. His wife and children rejoiced with him over the remarkable flowers, for they too discovered that the sight of them delighted the eyes and the smell of them refreshed the soul.

So as not to lose this treasure when the blossoms died the man planted them in a small plot of land behind his house. Sunlight and water kept the amazing flowers alive, still performing their marvelous magic.

When his children came to play in the yard, the man cautioned them against carelessness and wild play lest they trample the flowers and damage them. But the flowers remained hearty and strong so long as there was enough sun and moisture to nourish them.

Nowhere else could the man, his wife, and children find such remarkable solace from weariness, such comfort in sadness, such spiritual nourishment as these remarkable flowers provided. Here was a treasure beyond value.

As the family grew and more children came to play in the garden, the more concerned the man became over his remarkable flowers. To protect them he built a high wall around them. In time, because of his many children, he would allow them entrance to the small sanctuary, but only sparingly and then only with numerous precautions.

Unfortunately, this began to cause consternation among the family members. In time, when the children caused their father stress or anguish, he would refuse them access to the garden and the flowers. Eventually he set up rules concerning who could enter the sanctuary, how they had to enter, and what they could do while there. For his part, he continued to see to it that his treasure received enough sunlight and water so that the flowers continued to perform their wondrous magic.

As grandchildren began to appear, the man felt even greater need to safeguard his treasure. Now access to the flowers became even more restricted. Requirements had to be met and standards upheld. Offices were established to judge worthiness and determine accessibility. It became necessary to have lawyers to defend, judges to weigh, guards to safeguard, caretakers to upkeep, and on and on.

The man's family, however, saw less and less of the flowers and experienced less and less of their magical powers. In the meantime, many of them went off by themselves in search of the flower lady. She was still out there — still giving away her amazing flowers.

~ 46 ~

The Fool

THE STORY IS TOLD that when the great artist Leonardo da Vinci finished painting his masterpiece the *Mona Lisa*, he went to the nearest tavern to celebrate his wonderful accomplishment, for a master always knows when he's seen a masterpiece.

While bantering and joking with his apprentices da Vinci noticed that many of the revelers were making sport of an ugly fool who was making his way from tavern to tavern entertaining the crowds for a spare coin or crust of bread. The fool was truly an ugly man, more troll than human. His eyes were far too small for his overlarge head, and his pupils came perilously close to bumping into one another. His ears were cauliflower and his nose a gourd. His mouth was locked in a perpetual grimace or smirk, depending upon the mood of the beholder. As the crowd raucously mocked him, a contentious rival artist hurled a challenge at the Master Painter.

"Leonardo!" he called. "You are a great artist. What say you? Can you make a silk purse out of this sow's ear?"

All eyes turned to the great man. This was no mere idle challenge, and everyone knew it. The Master must accept or forever be held in doubt.

He pondered only a moment as if to test the fidelity of the crowd. "Why not? If I can paint the most beautiful woman in the world I can make an Adonis of this Nature's fool. Return to this tavern after Vespers and the work will be complete."

When the Vesper bell finished tolling the tavern was filled to overflowing. The entire city of Florence had come to see what the great artist had done to the fool.

At last, da Vinci stood before the stage curtain and waited for the crowd to hush for the great unveiling. Would the fool's nose be Aquiline, some said, for surely that was the most noble of noses. Would his eyes be blue as the heavens, brown as the earth, or green as the grass on the hilltops? Would his mouth be gentle or firm?

In the midst of the din the Great One called for silence. A tentative and electric quiet came over the crowd. With an appropriate flourish the Master pointed to the curtain and proclaimed, "Behold the Masterpiece!"

Slowly the curtain drew back. The crowd as one body held its breath. The fool was seated on a stool facing them.

He was the same as before. Exactly the same. Not a hair was changed. Not an eyebrow plucked. There was silence. Only silence.

The rival artist called out. "The fool was too much a challenge even for the great da Vinci."

"Not so!" the Great One said. Then, pointing to the fool's face he said, "This face was painted by God, and only a fool would dare presume to improve upon the work of a Master."

~ Moral ~

A true Master recognizes a masterpiece
whenever he sees one.

47

A Special Little Garden

ONCE THERE WAS A MAN who had a little plot of land. It wasn't much, but it was enough for him. He was a busy man who had to work very hard because life was difficult. But he needed something to satisfy his spirit. So he decided to plant a garden on his little plot of land.

First, he grew flowers. Wonderful flowers whose vibrant colors gave promise to the spring; fragrant flowers that perfumed the long summer days; and warm, earthy flowers that softened the chill of impending winters. Later he planted evergreens that spoke of life in the midst of snow.

Over the years he continued to embellish his special garden, at one time planting trees that offered shade and beauty, at another time digging a small pond where his children could splash their feet and play with the fish. Finally, on the little land that was left he built a gazebo where he and his wife would while away the warm, summer nights. It was not much, but it was enough. It was a special little garden.

One day his neighbor died and left him the property adjacent to his. It was much bigger than his little plot of land. He immediately became fascinated by all the possibilities this new opportunity afforded him. So he set about making new plans. He would plant hedgerows and groves. He would create arbors with vine-covered trellises. He would build a huge pond for swimming in the summer and ice skating in the winter. His dreams became extravagant and the work would be consuming, but he set about the task with a firm resolve.

The little garden gradually grew bigger. The work took a great deal of what precious little extra time he had. Consequently, there was even less time for him to enjoy the beautiful new garden he was creating. And there was also less time and love for him to share with his wife and children. He consoled himself by thinking that there would be time enough for that when the new garden was finished. If he was going to do it, he was determined to do it right.

But in order to do it absolutely right he decided it needed a winding cobblestone road and a rolling fieldstone wall. A simple pond would no longer do. Nothing short of a romantic lake would suffice. Of course, this would require additional land, so he bought more.

With this much property he would need a new and larger home as a more fitting residence for so gracious an estate. There would have to be a carriage house for cars and a gate house to complement the decor. Since this was too much for him to do alone, he hired a team of laborers to do the work. Then in order to pay these laborers and buy all that was needed he had to work even longer and harder.

Unfortunately, he overextended himself. His energy drained, his resources ran out, and the work stopped. The stone wall was left unfinished. The lake became a swamp, and the garden was soon overgrown.

In his waning years, the man sat alone in his rickety, broken-down gazebo and dreamed of a little plot of land. Not very much. Just enough for him. And on this land he would have a very special little garden.

~ Moral ~

Where your treasure is, there also your heart will be.

48

Marvel Optician

A MAN FOUND HIMSELF wandering aimlessly through the streets of his native city, pondering deep within himself the purpose of his life and life in general. Of late, he had been growing steadily more confused and more frustrated with himself and the world around him. It was probably nothing more than mid-life crisis he was told, but that was hardly any consolation. Peace had become a distant memory and an impossible dream.

"I don't see anything I can do that I haven't done," he said, arguing with himself as his eyes filled with tears of frustration. Afraid that someone might see him talking to himself, he quickly glanced around. He squinted tightly to squeeze the water from his eyes, but his vision was still blurred. When he focused again, he found himself staring straight into the window of an optician's shop.

"Strange," he thought. "I've been down this street hundreds of times, and yet I've never noticed this shop before." The sign above the window read "Marvel Optician." The M of Marvel and the O of Optician were printed extra big and bright. There was something written beneath the sign, but the print was extremely small and difficult to read. "What a clever ploy to make people think they need glasses," he thought. He had to strain to make it out. It read, "Our glasses help you to see things differently."

"If ever anyone needed a pair of glasses to do just that it's me," he said out loud, not caring who might hear him. There was something very strange and intriguing about the place, so he decided to go in.

The shop was indeed a strange place. Instead of the usual row of display cases with an endless variety of frames, there was just one counter with three pairs of glasses lying on top of it. He was about to make a quick exit when the proprietor emerged from the door behind the counter. "How can I help you?" he said.

Not wanting to be rude but not wanting to show any interest in the foolish selection of glasses, he decided to make an idle comment and beat a hasty retreat.

"I've been in this neighborhood many times, and I've never noticed your shop before."

"That's probably because you weren't looking for it," he answered.

He half expected some commonplace reply after which he would have said something about just being curious and left, but what the man said was disarming. Then he realized that only moments before he had been squinting the tears out of his eyes and struggling to read the sign and surmised that the shopkeeper must have been watching him. However, he was in no mood to explain the tears to this stranger, so he simply said, "I'm not sure I know what you mean."

"If you need to see things better," he said, "then you're in the right place. If you're looking for just ordinary glasses, there's a regular optician a few blocks away."

"What's that supposed to mean?" he asked almost curtly, as if the man were playing with him.

"At Marvel Optician our glasses are different. They're special glasses."

"Is that why you have such a great selection?" he said cynically.

"When glasses do what ours do you don't need a big selection."

The man was definitely intriguing, he thought. And for a salesman he's got quite a line. Still he took the bait anyway. "What makes your glasses so special?"

The shopkeeper's eyes lit up. The pitch was sure to follow. Who knows if it works on me, he thought. I might even be willing to give this line a try myself.

"Our glasses don't just affect your vision, they affect your life."

The man was unbelievably clever. Every line he uttered had a double meaning. Everything he said begged further questions. The man was a genius. A truly master salesman.

"And what's that supposed to mean?" he asked, falling deeper into the trap.

"Our glasses affect your *modus operandi* (which he pronounced *oper-and-eye,* the way a fast talking traveling salesman would). Your M.O. It's Latin, son. It means the way you operate. M.O. Get it? Marvel Optician." Then he laughed.

At this he wanted to leave, but the man interrupted his departure. "That's why we're called Marvel Optician: because our glasses will change your life."

This was too much to bear. He picked up a pair from the counter and gestured like he was going to put them on. "You mean these glasses will change my life?"

"Not those," he said, reaching out to take them back.

"Why not these?" he challenged, holding them out of the proprietor's reach.

"Because they're children's glasses."

"What makes them children's glasses?" he asked, goading the man. "They look like just plain old ordinary glasses to me." He held them up and peered through the clear glass lenses without putting them on.

"They're not," he answered, seemingly unruffled. "They're fragile. Much too fragile for you. They will break extremely easily."

"Nonsense," he said and put them on. The moment he exerted a little pressure on them the frame broke and the lenses went crashing to the floor. He was immediately remorseful. It wasn't at all like him to be so belligerent. It must be because of the frustration he was facing in his life. He offered to pay for the damages and leave quietly. The proprietor was both kind and indulgent. "Not to worry," he said, and extracted another similar pair from beneath the counter.

Now he felt obligated to stay and buy something. Was this all part of the technique? He decided that no one could be that clever. Nonetheless he at least should try to look interested in the man's wares if for no other reason than to humor him.

He reached for another pair. Only this time he would put them on very carefully. As he did the owner said, "There is something I should tell you. While all my glasses are truly special, you may find something wrong with them."

"Now you tell me," he said, as he stood immobilized and awestruck by what he saw. Every color he looked at was brilliant. More brilliant and more vivid than he could ever remember. Every red was indescribably red. Every blue was infinitely blue. Every green and orange and yellow was luminescent. He was utterly fascinated and amazed. It was remarkable. All he could say was, "Wow!"

"I know how you feel," the owner said. "That's why we call those our Dazzlers."

Dazzled just barely described what he was feeling. Looking through the glasses made every fiber of his being seem to vibrate. Everything in him and about him was bursting with energy. He felt invigorated. He felt powerful. He could easily see how wearing these glasses could change his life, his *modus oper-and-eye*. And he wanted to.

"I want these glasses," he said.

"They're not right for you," the proprietor answered.

"What do you mean they're not right for me?" he shouted with more fire than he had felt in a long time.

"They're our adolescent model. They'll be much too much for you. You should have asked me before you put them on."

"I want them," he said stubbornly. "I must have them and I won't take no for an answer."

"Well, all right, if you insist, but don't say I didn't warn you."

The man rushed out of the shop never even giving a thought to paying for the glasses. He was much too excited about this new outlook he was experiencing. The world was awash in wonderful, brilliant colors. The trees were so real that it seemed like they would come right over and embrace him. The sky literally touched him all over, making his flesh tingle. Every cloud was a ball of cotton he could just reach out and squeeze. Everything had feeling. Everything stirred him down to his soul.

His body had become an antenna that vibrated at everything he saw through those special glasses. It was all very exciting. It was all very draining. After a while it was altogether too much. He went back to the shop.

"I see you've returned," the proprietor said, as if he had expected it all along. "I surmise you've discovered the flaw."

"If you mean that everything is too everything, you're right. What attracted me at first was what eventually undid me. Everything turned out to be simply too stark. Every color was so bright and vivid that I began to long for gentler shades and more muted tones. There were no pinks and beiges and grays. Everything was becoming more intense. Colors, sounds, emotions. I couldn't sustain it all any longer. I was exhausted."

"That's the problem with those glasses as wonderful as they are. But, then again, I did tell you that they were our adolescent model."

He looked compassionately at the hapless man. "Of course, we do have an adult model," he said, reaching for the third pair of glasses. "But it's only fair to warn you that while you'll see all the gentler shades of color, the reds will never be as bright again, or the greens as green, and the same for all the rest."

"Well, if that's the flaw of these glasses, it's one I can live with." When he put them on he found them much thicker and heavier than the others.

Unfortunately, it wasn't very long before he returned to the shop again. "You tricked me," he said accusingly, but without a great deal of passion. "You told me that the only flaw these glasses had was that I wouldn't see the bright colors quite so brightly again."

"I didn't say that," the shopkeeper replied. "You did."

Upon reflection he had to admit that the shopkeeper was right. He had simply presumed that the flaw was in the loss of vivid colors. But if that wasn't it, what was? Hadn't the man told him that there was something wrong with all his glasses? He asked himself what besides making everything dull and boring was wrong with the glasses. They had gotten heavier. He only gradually had become aware of that. But the question was were the glasses getting heavier or was he just getting older? Whatever it was he wasn't even curious enough to try to figure it out. Besides he had decided to just get rid of the glasses and leave.

When he went to take them off, he couldn't. They held fast as if stuck to his face. He tried again and again but it was no use. The glasses wouldn't budge. Then it dawned on him. He had discovered the flaw.

"So that's the flaw," he said, looking at the proprietor.

"Some people say that." Again an answer with a hidden meaning. The man was as engaging as he was frustrating.

"Do you mean that I'm stuck with these for the rest of my life?"

"I'm afraid so."

"You didn't tell me."

"I warned you."

"What do you mean?"

"I told you that you may find something wrong with my glasses. You should have looked before you leapt, if you'll pardon my pun."

"You mean that there's nothing I can do?"

The shopkeeper looked at him through compassionate eyes. "Not exactly."

"Now what's that supposed to mean?" He was in no mood for riddles.

"While it's true that you're stuck with those glasses, I do have something that can be done about them."

He was about to tell him to please refrain from the double-talk when the shopkeeper reached under the counter and brought out a cardboard shoe box. As he opened it he said, "I have a selection of clip-ons. You can have one of these if you wish."

Once bitten, twice shy, he thought as he warily looked through the selection. He held each pair up to the light and looked through it. Each seemed to be shaded differently — brown, blue, red, green, yellow, like sun glasses. But, he was not going to make any quick choice this time. He was going to be careful and shrewd. Besides he saw almost immediately the flaw in each clip-on. Each shade diminished all the other colors. However, there was one pair that captured his attention because they didn't seem to do anything. At least nothing he could see. He held them up for the proprietor to see.

"Those are my X.V. model."

"X.V.?"

"Extended vision."

The idea intrigued him. He could see no possible flaw in glasses that could give him extended vision. But just in case these didn't work out, he had a trick of his own up his sleeve this time. He clipped them on.

This time he returned quickly. He was disappointed and annoyed. "They didn't extend my vision at all as you claimed," he shouted. "Instead, they made me see spots before my eyes."

"Yes," the shopkeeper said.

"Spots everywhere. On the trees. On flowers. On buildings. On animals. On people. On the sky. On the ground. Everywhere I looked there were spots."

"If you see them, then they must be there."

"Is that more of your confounded double-talk? The spots can't be everywhere. I never saw them before."

"They were there. You just never noticed them before. The clip-ons simply helped you to see what was already there.

He was in no mood to play games with this man. He felt duped and irritated. "These clip-ons were supposed to give me extended vision. Extended vision, my eye, if you'll pardon my pun."

"They would give you extended vision if only you knew how to look at things."

"This time I did know how to look at things. So here's a surprise for you my friend. A flaw you missed. These glasses are clip-ons, which means I can take them off."

"That can be a flaw, . . . " he said stopping him momentarily. "If you don't use them the way they were meant to be used. The flaw, my friend, was never in the glasses, but in you. They will do what I said they would do. Haven't I spoken the truth to you throughout?"

He realized that the shopkeeper was right. He had spoken the truth, but it was done in that strange double-talk that oracles were said to use. He was told that the children's glasses were too fragile for him, and they'd break. So they did. He was told that the adolescent glasses were Dazzlers, and they had dazzled him. He was told that the adult glasses would not be as bright, and when they weren't he complained. But they did make him see the different shades of life. As a matter of fact they each affected the way he looked at life and the way he lived. They had affected his *modus operandi* just as he was promised. Everything thus far had been as he was told — except the clip-ons. Something was missing. He did not see how they could give him extended vision. All they gave him was spots. Spots. Could it be the spots? Was there something about the spots? Was there something in the spots?

Outside the shop he walked up to the closest spot he saw. It was on a tree. He drew closer to it. There seemed to be a dull glow about it. He had never gotten that close to notice it before. He had been too upset to even think of examining them. Now curiosity drew him closer. He could see that there was something odd about the spot. He felt strangely excited but unaccountably frightened. What would he see that would extend his vision? His nose was almost touching the tree.

Suddenly he drew back as if he had just been slapped. What he saw shocked him. It caught him completely off guard. It was the last thing in the world he would have expected to see. It was his face.

After he calmed down he approached it again. Sure enough it was his face. How could this be? What could it mean? He went over to another spot. This one was on a flower. He bent over and looked closely at it. Once again the spot revealed his face. He ran from place to place checking all the spots as each and every thing had a spot on it and every spot had his face in it. While it surprised and then delighted him he did not understand the phenomenon. How did this extend his vision?

Then the realization came. "I am a part of everything," he said. "I never knew that before. I never saw it before."

It was a marvelous revelation. What an incredible vision of life it gave him. This would unquestionably affect everything he did from now on. It would permanently change his outlook on the world. It would definitely change his *modus oper-and-eye,* he laughed.

It did change his life. He was happier than he had ever been before. He felt that everything in the whole world because it had his picture on it was his and a part of him. The clip-ons had done what was promised. They had given him extended vision just as the shopkeeper said. And the shopkeeper always told the truth.

Then why wasn't he satisfied? A niggling suspicion crept up the back of his neck. Something was wrong again. He sensed it more than knew it. The shopkeeper had also said that each of the glasses was flawed. What could possibly be wrong now? When he thought about it, he was shocked that he hadn't seen it sooner. If everything had a spot on it and every spot had his face in it, what would other people who got the clip-ons see? He wasn't so naive as to think that this would only happen to him. He felt utterly dismayed. He must examine the spots again. He went outside where the sunlight was bright and approached a spot. This time he didn't stop when he saw his face. He got even closer. He put his face hard up against it.

When he saw what he saw he began to laugh. "Of course," he said. It was the only possible answer. The spot was a mirror. Everyone would see himself in the spots. How could it be otherwise.

He had to go to the optician shop and tell the proprietor the good news. He hurried there only to find the shop closed. Disappointed at not being able to share his discovery, he started back. As he passed the window he decided to look inside. The glare of the sunlight on the window made him squint as he approached. The now familiar spot was immediately in front of him. He tried to look past it to the inside of the shop, but he couldn't. So he decided to look through it. He looked more closely at his reflection. It kept him from seeing beyond. He had a strange and desperate need to see the shopkeeper, to look beyond his reflection. Only the darkness of his reflected pupils offered the hope of looking beyond. He stared into them and blocked out everything else. He concentrated agonizingly hard to block out the sunlight and his reflection.

Then it happened. He was beginning to see beyond. Only he wasn't looking inside the optician's shop. He was looking even beyond that to what seemed like a tiny speck of light in the far distance. He sharpened his attention and narrowed his focus to that and only that. He suddenly felt drawn into the light's magnetism. It drew him deeper and deeper, faster and faster into the very core of its being, into the very heart of the light itself. Finally, he was bathed in light, awash in brilliant incandescence. Every darkness, every shadow, every imperfection and fault seemed to burn away. But there was no pain. Only joy. And lightness. An inexpressible lightness. The lightness of being. He was becoming so one with the light that he himself had become light. He was a living flame.

When finally he emerged from the experience he discovered that the clip-ons were gone. The glasses were gone. The Marvel Optician shop and its proprietor were gone. And he understood why. He had looked into the very eye of God. There would never again be flawed glasses for him to look through. From now on he could see forever.

~ *49* ~

The Moving House

To WHAT SHALL I COMPARE this generation? It is like a man who stood at the door of a house and knocked. A voice from within answered, "Enter."

When he opened the door he was struck by what he saw. Everything inside the house was moving. The walls moved. The floors moved. The ceiling moved. The furniture, the rugs, the lamps, the pictures — everything moved.

Some of the walls moved upward like shades, changing colors, designs, and textures. Some moved downward in contrasting designs and shapes. The ceilings moved in different directions as if they were on rollers in an endless array of differing patterns. The floors were like treadmills large enough only for one or at most two standing side by side. These paths moved at different speeds and in different directions. Furniture changed fabrics, pictures changed scenes, and tables changed styles. It was fascinating. Mesmerizing.

At first he just stood there in awe at this great marvel. Eventually he felt compelled to enter the house. He stepped onto the nearest treadmill and let it take him wherever it was going while he simply reveled in what was happening. The house was immense, and he traveled a long way moving from room to room. Sometimes he jumped onto different walks that took him in different directions through different rooms. Nothing ever remained the same.

In the midst of his wanderings he discovered that there were other people moving through the house with him. Sometimes they passed close by and he would begin conversations with them. This never lasted long since the paths would change abruptly and move in different directions or at different speeds, and they would move out of sight of one another.

At times when he craved company he would jump onto someone else's walk and they would converse. But he had no way of knowing how long this would last, since the walks would sometimes split and his partner would move off in another direction. Nor was eating a simple matter, for the chair he sat on and the table he ate at were both continuously moving and not always in the same direction or at the same speed. He would eat what food he could as best he could before things changed and moved off again. Even sleep offered no real respite, for as the bed moved so did the clock, but far more rapidly than he wished, and in no time at all he was back on the treadmill moving in directions he didn't always have control over.

What was at first a lark, soon enough became a tiring chore. Nothing was steady. Nothing was permanent. His whole being began to cry out for everything to stop. His soul craved stability. He had to get out.

Moving from walk to walk, jumping frantically, searching desperately to find a way out, he eventually made his way to the front door. Without even a look back he flung it open and threw himself outside.

He found himself on solid ground. It was wonderful. Wonderful not to move. Wonderful to rest and be at peace. He cried out, "At last, I have found a place that does not move!"

"That is not so," said an old man who suddenly appeared from nowhere. "For the earth is moving too."

"Then there is no hope," said the man.

"Not so," repeated the old man. "For out here where God rules, we all move together in the same direction at the same time."

~ 50 ~

The Legend of the Sacred Key
of St. Peter

ONCE UPON A TIME a young pilgrim was making his way back
to his north country home after having completed a holy pilgrimage
to the tomb of St. Peter in Rome. The fervor of his renewed faith
sustained him during his difficult trek over the mountains, but the
effort left him pitifully weak and sick when he arrived at a place called
the Garden of Birch Trees. He sought refuge among the people who
lived there, but they feared for their lives and for their goods and
would have nothing to do with strangers — pilgrims or otherwise.
Christians they were, they said, so they did him no harm. But fools
they were not, so they bade him off without food to strengthen him
or a cloak to warm him.

Wracked as he was with hunger and fever the young man felt certain he would die as he stumbled into a small mountain cave and
slumped to the ground. Was this to be his final resting place? Was his
great pilgrimage of devotion to end in so hapless a way? His noble
heart would not allow him to make his peace with God while lying
down so he struggled to his knees to offer his final prayer. The setting sun found the cave entrance and warmed his Nunc Dimittis —
"Now You may dismiss your servant, O Lord." When he finished his

prayer and opened his eyes he saw in a niche above his head an object gleaming in the sunlight. With a desperate effort he reached up and grasped hold of it. It felt strangely warm to the touch. It was a key. Its warmth was somehow consoling as he clutched it tightly and collapsed in a heap on the cave floor.

"A key to a rich merchant's treasure," he thought, "hidden here for safe-keeping. And I have no strength left even if I wished to claim the prize." Or, perhaps, it was the key to some fat farmer's larder filled with smoked hams and turkey and pheasants. The young pilgrim thought he surely must have died and was suffering the torments of purgatory. Well, at least, he had the consolation of knowing that it would end in heaven.

When he awoke he found that he wasn't in heaven. Fear clutched his heart. Was he is hell? But no! The aroma that enveloped him was of roasting rabbit, and unless there were rabbits in hell he felt certain that he was still very much alive. He had been found by a holy hermit who carried him to his humble hut and nursed him through his fever and delirium.

"You must feel no rancor toward these people, my son," the monk said after the young man had eaten and told his story. "Here at the edge of Christendom they are barely more than pagans. There is still too much fear in them." The young pilgrim surprisingly felt no anger at all toward them, only warmth. Warmth — there was a strange warmness in his hand. He discovered that still clutched in his grasp was the key he had found in the cave. He had forgotten about it. He imagined that it had just been the illusion of a dying man. But it was no fantasy. It was real and he could feel every part of the key in his closed grip.

For a moment he was tempted not to tell the hermit about it. After all, if it did unlock a treasure, it was rightfully his. Besides, what need would a holy monk have of earthly treasure? Still, he owed his life to the good hermit and conscience spurred him to confess all to him.

Nothing could have prepared him for the holy man's strange reaction. At first, he seemed to give the account only passing interest. But as the young man continued, he fell to his knees, repeatedly signing himself with the sign of the cross. Finally, he cried out, "Where is the key, my son?"

The young man opened his clenched fist and held it out. An eerie glow seemed to envelop it, just as it did when he first discovered it in the cave. Then it was the setting sunlight that it captured. Was it now trapping the glow of the fire in the hearth? His wonderment was stopped short as the monk threw himself prostrate on the earthen floor. The boy thought he had fallen in a swoon, but the mumbled prayers assured him that the hermit was quite conscious. However, he could neither rouse nor distract him, so he reverently waited for him to finish.

"What is it? Why did you carry on so?" he asked.

"My son," the monk whispered, "I believe you have found the sacred key of St. Peter."

What key of St. Peter? He had heard nothing of it during his pilgrimage in Rome. Surely he should have heard something about it while he was there. He might have dismissed the statement as the rambling of an old man except that he knew that the hermit had all his wits about him. He looked at the key carefully. It was a strange key, shaped in the form of the letter "T" like a cross, but unlike those he was accustomed to seeing. It still glowed faintly but that was simply because of the fire and not for some supernatural reason. But the strange warmth was still there. Could it not be just from his hand that clutched it so tightly. Still, he was intrigued.

"I have never heard of any key of St. Peter," he said. He held it out for the monk to examine, but the old man would not touch it. So he laid it gently on the table as he would a sacred relic. The monk stared at it for a long time before he finally explained.

"My son, are you familiar with the account where our blessed Lord told St. Peter, "I give you the keys of the kingdom of heaven. Whatever you bind on earth will be bound in heaven and whatever you loose on earth will be loosed in heaven"?

"Of course!" the young pilgrim replied, "But surely he spoke metaphorically. He gave him no actual keys."

"True enough," the old monk said. "But wisdom teaches us to go beyond the words to the meaning — a meaning that Peter himself was not to learn until after he had thrice denied him."

The young man was not yet old enough or wise enough to understand what the monk meant, so he listened closely.

"My good young man, tell me what binds people on earth?"

"Chains," he answered all to quickly.

"True enough. Chains and fear. But only for a while." The pilgrim blushed at this hasty reproof.

"What binds people permanently?" he continued.

This time the youth thought for a long time. "Only love binds people permanently," he exclaimed.

"Well said!" the old man smiled for the first time. "It is love that binds God's kingdom on earth to that in heaven."

"Yes, but what has that to do with this key?" The impetuosity of youth burned within him.

"Recall the scripture again. "On the evening of the first day of the week, although the door of the room was locked for fear of the Jews, Jesus came and stood in their midst. 'Peace be to you,' he said to them. Then he spoke once again of binding and loosening." The old man paused to let this new scripture sink in, but the young man could still not fathom the monk's meaning.

"I don't understand," he cried impatiently.

"The room was locked," the hermit said slowly to stress the point. "Who held the key to the upper room?"

"Peter, I suppose, as head of the Apostles."

"Think now, why was the door locked?"

"Because of their fear of the Jews."

"Just so!" the monk exclaimed and waited.

The young man fell into a deep and thoughtful silence. Then it came to him, and he cried out, "The door should not have been locked! Fear bound him. St. Peter had lost faith. Could that be possible?"

"Yes!" the old man shouted excitedly. "Christ came for a last time to restore his faith and set them free." He paused and then revealed the mystery. "The key was the symbol."

"Yes, I see it now," the youth exclaimed.

The holy hermit continued. "From that day on Peter kept the key with him wherever he went. Fear would never again bind him. He would never again lock a door. His threefold pledge of love had set him free. The key went with him to Rome, and Rome was eventually unlocked and set free."

The young pilgrim was thrilled that he was sharing in this wondrous mystery. But still more of it remained. He puzzled for a moment and then asked, "How did the key come to be in this place if indeed this is the key of St. Peter?"

"Legend has it that the key was kept by the successors of Peter. However, during the persecutions it was lost. It was rumored that Constantine the Great came upon it and set loose pagan Rome. Christ and love triumphed and Christendom was born. The legend claims that whoever finds the key and uses it with love will set captives free and be called great in the kingdom of heaven.

"But then tragedy struck in the person of Attila the Hun. After he ravaged Rome he was rumored to have taken the key back with him to Germany. But on the way it was lost. "My son," the monk paused to look directly at the youth, "this place was on the route Attila the Hun took on his journey back."

"Could it be," the young pilgrim wondered reverentially, "that this is actually the sacred key of St. Peter?"

"There may be a way to discover the truth," the old man offered as if reading his thoughts. "Many years ago I was sent off by a successor of our holy founder Benedict to found a community in the north country. The journey over the mountains was too much for my frail body to bear, so I settled here instead of in my intended destination. He gave me letters and documents to present when I arrived, but somehow I felt drawn to remain here as a hermit. All these many years I have struggled to understand God's will in this, but could not. Can this be the reason?"

The old man knelt at his cot and reached beneath it. He withdrew a small chest, old, weather-worn, and rusted. "I have long since lost the key," he said, "but it made no difference to me since I was fated never to go beyond this point." He handed the chest to the youth, who took it with trembling hand.

He placed the box on the wooden table where he had laid the key. When he picked up the key it was still warm. Suddenly, his fear left him. He was confident and full of faith. He placed the key in the lock and turned it. The chest opened.

The youth cried out jubilantly, "It worked! It's open! It's open."

He looked happily at the old man. Instead of sharing his excitement the hermit seemed stolid and pensive. Still, his eyes betrayed him. They were wet with tears.

"Why are you not rejoicing with me old man?" the youth barked.

"That is not the test, my son," he whispered.

The boy was struck dumb confounded! Then he cried out, "What do you mean? The key opened the chest. See!" He held out the open chest to reassure the holy hermit.

"That is not the test," he repeated. He paused an eternity and sighed, "Now you must see if it can lock it again."

The boy looked at him quizzically. Why would he have to lock it again? After all, it has passed the test, the chest was opened. Fear gripped him. He was afraid to try again. Fear. "Fear binds," he remembered the old man saying. He must not lose faith. Not now. Not when so much suddenly depended on it. He grasped the key firmly, put it back into the lock, and turned it. There was no click. He turned it again. Still no click, no tumblers falling to place. He turned it again and again, but it refused to lock. His head sagged. His chest fell. The breath of life seemed to go out of him.

"It didn't lock," he stammered. "It didn't lock."

The old man's face suddenly beamed with a glow that rivaled the sun.

"Praised be Jesus Christ!" he shouted. "Praised be Jesus Christ!" he repeated over and over again. Then he fell to his knees and prayed. "Now you may dismiss your servant in peace, O Lord, for my eyes have seen the salvation which you have prepared for all nations, a light of revelation for the gentiles and for the glory of your people, Israel."

"What is it?" the astounded youth cried to him. "What's happened. It didn't lock. It failed the test."

"No, my son. It didn't fail," the old man wept with joy. "It passed the test. The door to the upper room can never be locked again. This key only opens. It never locks. It is the sacred key of St. Peter. It is the key. It is the key," he repeated again and again until it filled the humble hut like a chanted litany.

The next day the young pilgrim set out for his journey home. Before he left, the old hermit gave him a blessing. As he entered the birch forest, the holy monk called out to him, "Tell me, my son, before you go, what is your name?"

"My name, holy father," he shouted back as he waved good-bye, "is Charles."

The young pilgrim grew up to be a great man according to the legend of the key of St. Peter. He became Charles the Great, better known to history as Charlemagne.

But the legend does not end since the key cannot be destroyed. Time and again, down through the centuries great individuals have emerged and loosened bonds and set captive peoples free. During the great wars of Europe, the key found its way to the Americas, where it was rumored to have been discovered by one Martin Luther King, Jr. Having done its work there, it made its way back to captive Europe, where it was chanced upon by a Lech Walesa; thence it journeyed to South Africa where it was smuggled to a prisoner named Nelson Mandela. The last that was heard of the sacred key, my friends, was that a monk was carrying it home with him to his native land of China.

 God Is Love

God is love means that
you don't have to do anything
to make God love you,
and you can't do anything
to make God stop loving you.

 Miracles and Signs

Everything stops at a miracle.
Nothing stops at a sign.
Miracles are meant to be signs that point ahead.

~ 51 ~

Lions' Fare

"**L**ET US FEAST!" said the pride of lions over a recent kill.

"All I want is the thigh," said one lion. "I too would like a thigh," said another. Several others also preferred the thigh, so they formed a group called the Thigh Eaters.

When others of the pride saw this, they each began calling out the part of the kill that they wanted.

"I want the shank." "I want the ribs." "I want the rump." And so on.

These too divided up the kill according to their desires and were designated as the Hip Eaters, the Shank Eaters, the Rump Eaters, and so on.

Thus, the feast was divided between many groups. When the Thigh Eaters sat down to eat, some of them called out, "I want the left side of the thigh." Others wanted the middle of the thigh, and still others the right side. They too split their part of the meal and divided themselves into the Right Side of the Thigh Eaters, the Middle of the Thigh Eaters and so on. So too did the Shank Eaters and the Rump Eaters divide themselves.

When the Right Side of the Thigh Eaters sat down to feast, some among them said, "I want the part with no bones." Others wanted the part with bones, so they further divided themselves into the Right Side of the Thigh with No Bones Eaters and the Right Side of the

Thigh with Bones Eaters. Of course, the same was demanded of the Middle of the Thigh Eaters and the Left Side of the Thigh Eaters so that they were divided into Middle of the Thigh with No Bones Eaters and the Left Side of the Thigh with Bones Eaters and the like.

You would think that by this time they were hungry enough to eat anything. They were, but unfortunately there were still other distinctions that they insisted upon before the feast could begin. The pride further split themselves and the meal into with or without skin, with or without hair on the skin, and so on.

They never finished dividing and splitting among themselves. Not that it would have made any difference for the jackals had run off with the prize.

 Stereotypes

*We would do well to remember that stereotypes
are born from observation and not imagination.
Nothing will put the lie to a false stereotype
better or faster than the truth.*

52

The Special Meal

A MAN AND A WOMAN loved each other very much. They wanted to celebrate their love in a very special way so they decided to do it in a meal. Not just any meal. Only a full-scale banquet could express the depth and scope of their deep love for one another.

So they immediately began to plan it. Only the best of dishes would be suitable for such a celebration. Since what they had was inappropriate for anything but ordinary, everyday meals, they went out and purchased a set of fine imported bone china.

Now one could hardly expect them to put common knives and forks alongside such exquisite plates, so next they bought elegant new silverware.

In such a setting could anything but leaded glass crystal goblets suffice? Of course, there just had to be silver candelabras to finish it off.

The place setting was now a thing of beauty. But the table wasn't. You simply couldn't put such an elegant setting on an ordinary table. A carved oak table with hand-wrought captain's chairs was needed. And to complement that there just had to be a beveled-glass buffet and an oriental sideboard.

What else could they do to accommodate such splendor but have the floors refinished or newly carpeted and have the entire dining room wallpapered. Finally, not just the place setting but the entire room was a thing of beauty, a jewel.

Unfortunately, it seemed cast in a pauper's setting. There was no other recourse but to have the entire house remodeled. So the living room was refurnished, a den was added, wall-to-wall carpeting was laid throughout the entire house, the upstairs bedrooms were redone, the exterior got new siding, and a landscaper sculptured the grounds outside.

Finally, everything was ready for the special meal. Unfortunately, they had no more money left for food.

~ Moral ~

First things first.

 ### Morsel or Banquet

*A morsel eaten in peace and with freedom
is greater than a banquet with strings attached.*

 ### Money

Money is the devil-s-tool.

53

The Parable

While traveling through Europe a young man stopped for a brief sojourn in Sicily. He arrived in late spring at the time of the harvest of a native fruit known as naspoli. It is a small fruit, about the size of a quarter, that tastes like a cross between an apricot, plum, and orange. If it is plucked and eaten at the optimum point of ripeness it is indescribably delicious. The locals say it is honey from heaven. The young man was so captivated by its taste that he determined then and there that he would take the fruit back to America with him. The farmers told him that the fruit did not travel well, otherwise they themselves would have long since provided it for export. Undissuaded, he carefully packaged some of the fruit and flew home.

Before he gave some to his family and friends, he regaled them with a tantalizing account of his wonderful discovery. Finally, he gave one to each of those assembled and they ate. It was truly good, but no longer indescribably delicious. The farmers had proven right. The fruit did not travel well. He made frustrated attempts at explaining how much tastier it really is when picked and eaten at its prime, but the proof of the pudding is in the eating. Some of his friends made no more of it than an exaggerated fish story and left it at that. Others believed him and wanted to know what could be done about growing the fruit locally. When he inquired, he was told that previous attempts had been made and failed. His only recourse would be to provide a greenhouse and duplicate all the conditions of its native habitat. On a large-scale basis this was obviously much too costly for a commercial venture, but a few well-tended trees just might succeed.

After much time, work, and expense everything was finally in readiness. The young man planted the seed and carefully provided for its growth. Since the mature tree took years to develop, he continued on with his life, getting married and raising children. His whole family waited patiently to taste of the fruit of his many years of effort. When the tree at last came to flower, only a few blossoms survived the ordeal and came to fruit. At precisely the right moment of ripeness he picked the fruit and gave one to each member of his family. His efforts had proven successful. The fruit was indescribably delicious. It truly tasted like honey from heaven. He had passed on the gift to those he loved, but he was not satisfied. He urged his children to do what he had done and to continue the tradition.

Some of them felt that the effort involved was just too much for them. Besides, there were other fruit. Admittedly, they could not compare to the naspoli, but they were tasty nonetheless and could be had for little or no effort. Some of his children made attempts, but the wait and effort eventually did them in. Their trees wilted and died without leaving any seed. He implored his last child not to abandon her efforts. She grew her own tree, not just out of love for her father, but because she had tasted that marvelous, unduplicatable fruit and wished her children to have the same.

~ Moral ~

The fruit is the kingdom of God.

54

Whatever Happened to the Party?

A meditation on how a retarded person sees the church.

I'M INSIDE. It's warm and I feel good. I can't see anything yet but it doesn't matter because I can hear. Everybody's happy about me. Everybody wants me. There's going to be a party for me when I get out. Okay! You want me to come out, so I'll come out.

~

Well, I like that! If you're so happy about seeing me, why are you spanking me? I haven't done anything...yet.

~

How come the doctor's so upset? Is it because I won't cry? Would it make him happy if I did cry? I don't think so. My Mommy's crying and he's still not happy. There's my Daddy. I don't know if he's happy, he's just not talking. Where is everybody? There was supposed to be a party when I came out and nobody's here. I think I'll go back.

~

Now everybody's happy. Everybody hugs and kisses me. I like that. I must be Italian. They say I'm Mongoloid. What nationality is that?

I like everybody, even my sister and brothers. Well, most of the time. But three of them is about all I can handle.

We go to church. I like church. I like the parade when the service starts. I want to march too. I like the smell of incense. It smells like Daddy in the morning. I like when the priest sprinkles us with water. He's like Mommy watering flowers. When the water hits me in the face, will it make me grow? Next time I come I'm going to wear my raincoat. When I get home I'll ask Daddy if it's okay. He doesn't go to church anymore. He still doesn't talk much, either.

~

I think my brother's sick. Mommy says he's got CCD.* But I don't have to worry. Mongoloids don't get it.

Church isn't as much fun as it was before. Oh, it starts out with a parade.† An even bigger one than before. But they won't let me march in it. I like the guitars too, only I can hear the organ better. Nobody sings much either. Maybe it's because the songs have too many words to remember. Daddy would like it if nobody sang. He's still not talking much. He still doesn't go to church. I think he's mad at God about something.

~

I want to go to communion. The priest says I can't because I don't have IQ. Is that like CCD? I don't have that either. He told Mommy that I don't have reason. I do so! My reason is because everybody else gets communion. Why not me? Besides, he says I have to go to reconciliation first. Where's that? Is it as far as Boston? Daddy's not talking at all, again. I think he's mad. Whatever happened to the party?

They brought me to my new home. I don't like it. They said it's

---

*CCD stands for Confraternity of Christian Doctrine and is used by Catholics to signify religious education.

†The entrance processional got bigger after the Vatican Council.

the best place for "us." If it is, why isn't my family coming with me? Who's "us" if not my family? They say I have a new family now. Well, it's too big if you ask me. But nobody asked me.

Why is this better? Two brothers and a sister was about all I could handle before. Now there's twenty of us in my room. Besides, this ain't a house like my house. It's too big. They call it an institution. That's not a house.

I'm supposed to have a new Mommy. She wears the same clothes all the time. My real Mommy dresses different all the time. Everybody wants my new Mommy's attention. You know how tough that is when there's twenty of us? I don't care because they tell us that in the institution we really got three sets of Mommys and Daddys — from seven in the morning until three in the afternoon; from three in the afternoon until eleven at night; and from eleven night until seven in the morning. Having three sets of Mommys and Daddys gets confusing. It's a little tricky trying to remember which one wants what from you. But that's not all. You see, then there's a ward charge and a supervisor who comes around to straighten all of them out. Then there's the teacher at school and the teacher's aide. And still that's not all! There's the social worker, the psychologist, the occupational therapist, the physical therapist, the doctor, the recreation specialist, the workshop supervisor, foster grandparents, and volunteers. Thank God, I'm Mongoloid. My brothers and sister could never handle all this. They're Italian.

~

I'm going to a group home. I'm glad. Only my new neighbors aren't. I wonder why? They haven't even met me yet. It's better in the group home. It's more like my real home. It's easier. But nobody ever hugs me anymore.

~

I go to a real church again. I get envelopes. I must belong. I can't wait to tell Monsignor that Susie and me want to get married. Boy! Will he be surprised.

~

Well, Susie and me are just living together. I want to tell everybody that she's my wife. I feel so proud, so grown up. We get kinda lonely. We go to church every Sunday like everybody else. And we go to communion every Sunday like everybody else. But we go home alone. For a while we used to have people who called themselves an Encounter Couple visit us. It was wonderful. It made us feel grown up like them. We would sit in the living room and have coffee and cookies. We wanted to make a Marriage Encounter weekend, but we couldn't. We're not married.

~

We still go to church. We still get envelopes. But I don't put anything in them.

~

Susie's sick. The doctor did all he could do. They told me to see the priest. I went to the rectory. Monsignor and the young priest had an argument about us.

~

The funeral was nice. A lot of people came. Even though it was sad, it felt good to get so much attention again.

~

I still go to church. Father lets me help the janitor. I like weddings the best. Everybody's all dressed up and they all stand there like pretty, dressed-up dolls. Especially the girls. They giggle and they cry. The guys look over at them and give the eye. You know. Cause they know that pretty soon the bride and groom are going to do it. Because that's what marriage is all about. That's what Father said to me and Susie. And having kids, and a family, and Christmas. But we never had any kids cause I'm Mongoloid and I can't have a family. If I could I'd show them how to have a real family. Anyway, Susie's gone. And nobody ever hugs me anymore. I'm getting to be like my Dad. I don't talk much anymore.

~

I haven't been feeling very good lately. They say it's because I'm getting older. I'm not really that old. Besides, I don't feel old. Anyway, I'm all alone and lonely a lot. I don't care if I die. But before I die I'd just like to know one thing. Won't somebody please tell me, whatever happened to the party?

 Saying Things Right
When people don't want to hear what you have to say,
there's no way to say it right.

 In the Land of Blind Men
In the land of blind men
is the sighted man guilty of sin for seeing?

Prayer

A FARMER AND HIS NEW WIFE stood gazing wistfully at their land. "One day," the woman said, "I would like a son and have him marry and move onto the land next to us in this valley."

The farmer knew that the land she spoke of was not good for farming as it had no water. So he proceeded up the mountain to the lake that fed the rivers that fed the valleys, and he dug a trench. Over the years the trench became a run-off, then a stream, then a rivulet, and finally a river that watered the land adjacent to the farmer's land.

When his son was ready to marry, he told his mother, "The land next to ours is well watered and fertile. My wife and I will settle there close to you."

~ Moral ~

Before the world began God heard our prayers
and dug a trench that set in motion a stream
that has been flowing for countless millennia
to water the land for those we've prayed for
if they choose to live there.

~ *56* ~

The Silver Rose

ONCE UPON A TIME, a beautiful young princess was walking through the royal gardens at dusk when suddenly she saw a silver rose. It was so unlike all the other flowers in the garden with their warm vivid colors of red, yellow, green, blue, and even white that she was immediately attracted by it. It was a bright and beautiful flower and its fragrance was ever so delicate. There was no other rose in the entire garden just like it, nor had she ever seen one before. She hurried to the castle to tell her mother, the queen, of her remarkable discovery.

"Where did such a beautiful and delicate rose come from?" she asked.

The good and wise queen told the princess the story of the silver rose.

"Once, at the beginning of time, when God was creating all things, God made the sun and saw how good it was. It was warm and bright and beautiful. 'I am beautiful,' the sun said to all the other stars, who twinkled back in agreement.

"One day, the sun in a moment of vanity wanted to see just how beautiful it was, so the sun made a mirror, the moon, and held it up to its face. 'Yes, indeed! I am very beautiful,' the sun said, admiring its reflection. Now God would not have any of His creation be vain so He made the earth and put it between the sun and the moon. God did this to humble the sun, and that is exactly what it did. Instead of adding to its vanity by reflecting it, the earth took it away by absorbing it. In return the earth gave back to the sun by bringing forth all kinds of wonderful things. Among them are the flowers. During the day when the sun shines, the flowers open up to receive its light and warmth. They then show their gratitude by wafting sweet fragrances toward the sun. Then at night when the air chills, they close up again to save their warmth for another morning or else they would freeze."

"But what about the silver rose?" the princess asked.

The queen continued. "Now the moon was born out of the sun's vanity and inherited that tendency itself. 'You have kept all the good things for yourself,' the moon complained, 'and have left me the night. I will claim what is yours.' So on certain nights the moon will shine brighter than at any other time of the month so that it can attract what belongs to the sun. It is on those nights that certain plants will bud and flower, thinking that they are doing so for the sun. Because they reflect the moon and not the sun, these are silver. They are rare and delicate and beautiful. They flower at dusk when others close and close at dawn when the others blossom. They give their beauty to the night only when the moon shines at its brightest."

The princess understood the story of the silver rose and made a special point of going out every evening at dusk just to see it. And because she knew about flowers, she did not pick it so that it could produce more lovely silver roses like itself. Thus was her disappointment so great when at the time of new blossoms there was no more silver rose. Again, she went to the queen.

"Why is there no other silver rose?" she asked.

"So it must be," the wise queen replied. "The silver rose has been deceived. It loves only the reflected beauty of the moon. Because of this, the sun is much too distant to give it warmth and color like the other flowers. And since she shows her beauty only at night, all the bees who would come courting are well into their rest awaiting another day. She blooms only for herself and the moon."

"Will there ever be another silver rose?" the princess asked.

"There most certainly will be others," the queen replied, "but one can never be sure when or where."

~ Moral ~

Vanity is doomed to be short-lived.
So too is false love.

 ### *Words to Remember*

When people don't thank you for what you've done,
they shouldn't criticize you for what you haven't done.

 ### *Exceptions*

There is wisdom in saying:
"Exceptions to the rule should not make the rules."

57

The Sage and the Seeker

A YOUNG MAN came before a great sage.

"What is it you seek?" asked the wise old man.

"I have discovered," said the boy, "that the greatest quest in life is the search for truth."

"What truth is it, then, that you seek from me?" the old man asked, furrowing his brow.

"I have a great fear that follows me day and night, everywhere I go. An ugly specter."

"It is your shadow," said the old man. "There is your truth."

"Call it what you will," the boy snapped impatiently. "I wish to be rid of it! It terrorizes my days and pursues me in my dreams at night."

"Come," said the old man.

He led the seeker to a cave.

"It is the cave of truth," he said. "Your quest lies within. Seek and find."

When, before long, the young man emerged, he found the sage seated at the mouth of the cave.

"Have you found the truth?" the old man asked.

"There was nothing there but darkness," the boy replied.

"What truth, then, did you discover?"

"I discovered that the shadow is not the body and the body is not the shadow, for in the darkness the body was there but the shadow was not."

"An illuminating truth," said the old man, furrowing his brow again.

"But the body cannot exist in darkness!" the boy cried in anguish.

Whereupon the sage gave the seeker a lighted candle.

"Enter again and find the truth," he said.

When the young man emerged, he found the old man waiting as usual.

"What truth have you discovered?" he asked.

"When I put the light before me, my shadow behind me was more fearsome than ever, for it was two and three times the very size of my body. But when I put the light behind me and my shadow came before me, I could not move, for I stumbled in its darkness."

"What truth, then, did you learn?"

"I must keep the light above me."

"Go and live your truth," said the sage. In time, the seeker returned again to the sage.

"Are you living your truth?" the wise man asked.

"I cannot!" the man cried. "For just as the shadow is not a part of the body, neither is the light. I cannot control the light!"

"Once again you have found truth," said the sage.

"But how do I live with it?" the seeker shouted.

"Live with what?" the sage asked. "The truth?"

"Not the truth! That I already have. How do I live with the shadow?"

"Ah! Then there is a greater quest in life than that for the truth," the old man said, unfurrowing his brow.

When, at last, the seeker returned to the sage a final time, there was a glow about him that radiated from deep within. And since it came from within, the shadow was now all around him. But he moved peacefully in the midst of it and took his place beside the wise old man.

58

The Boy by the Side of the Road

ONCE THERE WAS A GREAT COUNTRY immensely rich in natural beauty. Countless tourists were attracted to its majestic mountains, lush forests, and tropical beaches. However, while the land was rich, the people were poor.

One morning a tourist was driving through the countryside when he noticed a starving child lying at the side of the road. He was immediately moved to pity, but poverty was a commonplace sight in the destitute villages. Besides, he was on his way to a business meeting and was rushed for time. He placated his conscience by assuring himself that someone else who was less busy would soon come along and take care of him.

At midday, another tourist came along. The site of the poor child at the side of the road also moved him to pity, so he stopped. In the next moment, he thought about what his helping the child would entail. There would be questions at the hospital, involvement with the police and perhaps even the Department of Immigration and the U.S. Consulate. He might even have to extend his vacation, which was not possible. As much as he wanted to help, he really could not get involved. Without even so much as getting out of the car, he continued on his way, certain that someone else would come along and help the child.

At dusk, a third tourist drove by. When he saw the child he stopped the car and hurried over to him. When he saw the pitiful condition of the boy he was appalled at the sight of him. His hair was dirty and knotted; his clothes were filthy; his nose was running and he smelled awful. There was a stream nearby. He said to the child, "I have food in the car. I will get you some. Just go to the stream to wash up. When you return I will have something for you to eat."

On the way to the stream, the child died.

~ Moral ~

Real love is unconditional.

 ### *Righteous*

Righteous means to be set right.
This implies a certain humility
— the need to be set right —
which the righteous should not forget
once they've been set right.

 ### *The Test of a Man*

The test of a man is more in how he wields power
than how he obeys orders.

~ 59 ~

The Sculpture

A CHILD SAT PLAYING in his toy box. Bored with his vast selection of ready-made toys, he decided to build something on his own. He began with some alphabet and number blocks as a foundation. He added rings and springs and a host of other things. A sculpture began to take shape. He hadn't planned on making it permanent until he discovered that he could only go so far and all that he had done would come crashing down. Not wanting all his hard work to be in vain he began nailing, cutting, glueing, pasting, and doing whatever else was needed to help keep everything from falling apart. It really made no difference what he used or what he added — whatever was handy or simply struck his fancy.

"What is it?" his father asked.

"I don't know," he replied and continued playing.

All through his childhood and into adolescence he worked on his sculpture. He added a roller skate here and a hoola hoop there. Whatever fad or phase he passed through became a part of the collage. A bicycle seat, a pair of track sneakers, the garter from his first prom.

"What is it?" his father asked.

"I still don't know yet," he answered. "If I feel like doing this, I do it. If I feel like adding that, I add it. Whatever color or texture I feel like using, I use. It's kinda wonderful to be so free."

So the work continued and the sculpture grew. Over the weeks and months and years he kept adding on to it. Sometimes he worked on it like a hobby. Sometimes it was an obsession.

Every time he was asked, "What is it?" he responded, "I don't know."

Finally came the day when he decided to step back and take a good look at his creation. He studied it from every angle and every perspective, carefully assessing the totality of so many years of effort.

"What is it?" asked his now aged father.

"Nothing," he replied, and the sculpture collapsed under its own weight.

~ Moral ~

A house built on sand cannot stand.

 Dreams

Visionaries have dreams
and institutions pour them into concrete.

~ 60 ~

A Very Special Gift

H E WAS BRILLIANT. A genius actually. And he was an inventor. His son's twelfth birthday was approaching, and he wanted to give him a very special gift. Something that would last him a lifetime.

He decided to create for him a very special computer, one tailored just for him. Everything about it would be special and unique, just as his son was special and unique.

The finished product was truly a marvel. The machine would turn itself on at the mere sight of the boy or at his voice. He could either type into it or speak to it, whichever moved his fancy. The screen was the size of a blackboard on which he could create works of art, or he could sit back and be entertained while it did so at his command. It played music like a full symphony orchestra, formed pictures in three dimensions, and could create images out of the boy's memory. Of course, it also did all the normal things computers do from calculations and word processing to playing games.

He finished it just in time. He scoured around the garage until he found an appropriate box to put it in. His wife wrapped it with pretty paper, ribbons, and bows.

When the day finally arrived and the great unveiling took place, he seemed more excited about his creation than his son did, and he told his wife so.

"In time," she said understandingly.

The boy expressed only passing interest in the gift. What really attracted him was the box it was wrapped in. That had all kinds of possibilities. Cut out a few windows here and there and it was a house. Add some dentils along the top and it became a castle. A few modifications and it was a racing car. He played with the box for a whole year.

"When will he get to the computer?" he asked his wife.

"In time," she said understandingly.

But he continued to be fascinated with the box. All through his adolescence he monkeyed with it. Then into his young adulthood.

"When?" he asked his wife patiently.

"When he gets older," she said understandingly.

He never lost his compulsion for the box. His interest in it waned for a while, but at his fortieth birthday he became obsessed with it again as never before.

"When?" asked his father.

"Some day," said his mother. "I hope."

~ Moral ~

We pay more attention to the body than to the spirit.

 ### The Hardest Word

*The hardest word to accept
in an affluent society is "NO."*

~ 61 ~

That's Nice

ONCE UPON A TIME there was a great and powerful king who ruled over a vast and mighty kingdom. He was so great and so powerful that he was able to withstand the siege of time and the onslaughts of very powerful forces, either one of which had done in many another king.

Then, one day, what great kings and mighty forces could not do a simple little peasant girl did. He was defeated by love. As he was making his way through one of his many small villages his eyes fell upon a simple servant girl, and he fell immediately and irrevocably in love. His love for her was so sudden and so overwhelming that this mighty king's knees began to wobble so badly he could barely stand and his breath came in such short gasps that he could barely speak.

Now one would think that a girl to hold such power over him was some kind of a raving beauty but the truth was that she was no such thing. She was hardly beautiful, what with a wart on the end of her nose. But she wasn't ugly either. She was simply rather plain. For a king who could pick from among the many beautiful women of his court or the kingdom for that matter this was a strange choice. Then again, a servant girl, a peasant, was unquestionably beneath his station. He could do better. He should do better.

But, as everyone knows, love is blind, and when we are smitten we are powerless to do anything about it. Even though it happened so quickly, the king had fallen head over heels in love and he had to tell her.

"Well," the peasant girl said, "that's nice."

"I don't think you understand," the king said. "I'm madly and passionately in love with you."

"Well, that's nice," the girl said again.

"I don't think I'm making my point," he repeated. "I'm so desperately in love with you that I'll do anything you want. Ask me to swim the widest ocean and I will. Ask me to climb the highest mountain and I will."

"Well," she said, "that's nice."

Dauntless, the king continued. "How can I make you understand that I would give anything and everything I have for you. Ask me for rich jewels, and you have them. Ask me for magnificent clothes, and they're yours. Ask me for half my kingdom, and you've got it. Ask me for all my kingdom, and I will hand it over to you."

"Well," the peasant girl continued, "that's nice."

Frustrated, the king pleaded. "I will do everything I can to make you happy, if only you would marry me."

"Well, that's nice," she said for the umpteenth time.

The king could not understand her coolness and aloofness. Any fair maiden would have given a king's ransom and then some for his love, yet this plain peasant girl was not the least bit moved. Something was terribly wrong.

Finally, it dawned on him. He had been telling her what *his* love meant. He had not asked her what she might want. "Is there anything you want, my love?" he asked.

"I want to get rid of this damn wart on the end of my nose," she replied, without the slightest hesitation.

She had no sooner said it that the king reached over and kissed it. Immediately, it disappeared.

Now if, dear reader, you believe in fairy tales you would expect that the plain peasant girl suddenly became a raving beauty. But, in fact, this is not a fairy tale. It is a true life story. With the wart no longer preoccupying all her time and attention she was freed up to love the king. And she did.

When the wedding day finally arrived and she processed down the aisle to her anxiously awaiting bridegroom, she was truly not that much prettier than she was when the king first saw her even though she was adorned in a magnificent bridal gown and wore lavish jewelry.

But she was radiant. Love had made her so.

And the people of the kingdom said, "Well, that's nice."

~ Moral ~

True love is never self-absorbed.

 Losing Weight

> *Losing weight doesn't make you*
> *more handsome or more beautiful.*
> *It only makes you thinner.*

62

The Strange Weed

A MAN WENT OUT to grow a garden. He tilled the ground, planted seeds, and watered the soil. Eventually, small buds began to emerge. Unknown to him a strange weed also took root and began to grow. As the plants grew so also did the weed. When he noticed, it he paid it no attention as he had many more important things to do. He had yet to learn what all good gardeners know, that weeds deserve as much attention as plants. The weed grew quickly, sending out sprouts and shoots in every direction.

It was only when the weed had begun to choke off the plants and itself blossom into foul-smelling flowers that the man decided to take action. He grabbed hold of the stem to uproot it, but it had thorns and they punctured his flesh. The weed also had grown burrs that caught on to his clothing and tangled his hair. In addition it secreted a sticky substance that gave him a rash when he touched it. Finally, he had an allergic reaction to its pollen. Eventually, he took a pair of shears and went through the garden cutting away at the weed's many tentacles. He felt that he had finally rid himself of the pesty thing.

Unfortunately, as every good gardener also knows, a weed will continue to grow unless you kill it at the root. So the strange weed sent out even more shoots as it spread its roots underground. The dreaded thing began to crop up all over his property. The problem became too overwhelming for him to bear so he moved away.

At his new home, the man once again decided to grow a garden. He tilled the soil, planted seeds, and watered the ground. After a few weeks, tiny buds began to appear. So too did the strange weed. Without knowing it he had brought its seed with him.

~ Moral ~

Death is the weed.
Fear, pain, and anguish are its flowers.

 ## Pain

Pain is the body's way of saying something's wrong.
But why does it have to keep repeating itself?

 ## Fanatics

The driving force behind every fanatic is fear.

63

The Widget Maker:
A Fable about Old Age

ONCE THERE WAS A YOUNG MAN who came from a poor family. It was his great ambition in life to make something of himself — to rise above the slums and the poverty and to leave his mark on the world. He did this in a most unique and unexpected way. While puttering in his workshop one evening, he put together a widget. It was the first of its kind ever in the whole world.

The discovery thrilled him. He knew instantly that this was to be his great contribution. But first he would have to make people aware of it and convince them about how useful it could be to them. So he went among the poorer classes, since these were the people he knew and lived with. They were skeptical at first, but that was to be expected. After all, when you don't have much money you're not about to throw it away on some foolish invention. However, they were good people, so they helped him and bought his widgets. They were amazed and pleased at how useful and versatile they were. The women used them for all sorts of things around the house, while the men found them helpful at work. The word spread quickly, and there was a great demand for them.

He made his widgets day and night, selling them faster even than he could make them. So he hired others to work for him, and production began in earnest. Once the manufacture of widgets moved along smoothly, he set out to find new markets. Widgets weren't something that only the poor could use. The middle class could benefit from them too. Even the rich would be able to find a place for them. So he took the widgets to them, convinced all of them, and worked along with them. The production and sale of widgets grew to incredible proportions.

He married and his children joined him in the business. They all prospered, for widgets had become a national craze. Being president of a great company was no reason to rest on his laurels or join the idle rich. He was a drone — a sincere and honest hard-working man who never forgot his roots. He learned management, business technology, telemarketing, and labor relations. He grew and his business grew.

Then one day it happened. The fad ended almost as quickly as it began. The widget craze was over. The bottom fell out of the market, literally overnight. The widget empire crumbled and took everything with it — his stock, his security, his savings, his investments. Everything went.

After a life of hard work, he was poor once again. He who wished to make his mark on the world, who wanted to leave a fortune to his children, didn't have a farthing to his name. He was a failure. And he was too old to start again. He shut himself up from the world. He was a man without hope, a scion without a legacy. Or so he thought.

It was his grandchildren who taught him otherwise. They forced themselves into his isolation and invaded his solitude. "Tell us what you did, Grandpa?" they insisted.

Because he could not put them off and because he loved them, he told them his story. They sat there wide-eyed and all ears. Then they told others at school about his adventure and they too were fascinated. The teachers asked the old man to come in and speak to the students in Junior Achievement about what he had done. They too became fired up over what a poor immigrant boy could accomplish, so they began projects of their own. They asked him to guide and advise them. When their projects succeeded, he was asked to help the local college, and then the Chamber of Commerce.

On his seventy-fifth birthday, the community threw a luncheon in his honor. It was a pleasant occasion with civic and religious leaders, family, friends, and even former employees in attendance.

He was pleased with it all but was still sad as he walked home. He hadn't left a legacy to his children. He had no fortune to bequeath. He still considered himself a failure. Tears began streaming from his eyes, when suddenly he was startled by a boy who stepped into his path. He held up a grubby hand into the old man's face. He was holding something out to him.

"Hey, Mister!" he said. "Wanna buy a widget?"

~ Moral ~

The legacy of the old is not wealth but wisdom.

 ### *The Good Old Days*

The old days were good.
We would do well, however, to remember
that today is tomorrow's old day.

 ### *Reminiscences*

Reminiscing is truly valuable
when it shows what in the past
is worth looking forward to in the future.

~ 64 ~

The Time Princess

ONCE UPON A TIME a young princess seeking to fill some idle time went exploring about the family castle when she chanced upon a secret room in one of the castle towers. The room was filled with all sorts of strange and wonderful clocks. There were cuckoo clocks with pretty little birds that would pop out every half hour. There were animal clocks with big, bright eyes that moved back and forth, back and forth. There was a funny looking dog clock whose tongue moved in and out of its mouth. There was still another with a mouse that made its way up a pendulum only to fall back down when the clock struck one. There were hour glasses, sundials, and many, many other time-pieces, too bizarre even to describe. But in the middle of the room commanding all attention stood a majestic and stately grandfather clock.

The princess stood before it for a long time before she finally spoke.

"May I have a minute of your time?" she asked.

"Take two or more, if you like," the old clock said. "It's all that I have to give."

"Why is it that you tick tock? Always tick tock."

"I don't always," he said. "Sometimes I whirr and sometimes I buzz. At others times I might plod or slip or zip. It all depends."

The princess found the old clock interesting, if not amusing. "On what does it depend?" she asked.

"On what sound people give me," he answered. "Actually, I make no sound at all, you know."

"No, I didn't know," the princess said curiously. "Why do people give you a sound?"

"I suppose it's so that they'll know I'm here," he said and chimed the quarter hour.

The princess politely waited for him to finish and continued, "Are you always here?"

"Always," he answered.

"Well, I'm an intelligent girl," she said petulantly, "and if you're always here, I will certainly remember it, so you needn't make any sound at all as far as I'm concerned."

Spoken like a true princess.

The old grandfather clock stopped ticking. The pendulum swung back and forth silently. In fact, there was no sound at all from any of the clocks in the room. The princess made her exit.

~

Years later the princess returned to the silent room.

"Why must you pass so slowly?" she scolded the old grandfather clock.

"I don't pass slowly and I don't pass quickly," he said. "I just pass."

"I was told that one day I will be queen, but I want to be queen now! How long must I wait?"

"How can I tell you if I make no sound."

"Then by all means tick tock again, if you must," she demanded.

"It is not a must for me, but for you. So that you will know that I am here. That I am passing by."

"I am not often aware of you," she said impatiently. "Are you always here?"

"Always," he said.

"Then you had best let me know."

Once again the old clock ticked and tocked with every swing of its long pendulum. The princess stood there listening.

"Can't you go any faster?"

"I can't go any faster and I can't go any slower," he said. "I just go by."

~

Some time later the princess returned. "Today I am queen," she said imperiously.

"Congratulations!" the old clock said. "I knew it would come."

"I have waited long for this moment."

"That's not my fault," he sighed. "I tick tock the same for queen and peasant alike."

"But today is the fulfillment of all my dreams. I do not wish it to pass quickly."

"I can't go any slower or any faster today than any other day," he chimed. "I just go by."

~

Years passed. A doddering old queen returned to the room and stood once again before the grandfather clock.

"Where did the time go?" she sighed.

"I didn't go anywhere," he said. "I am always here."

She stood there a long while stooped over her cane listening to the gentle tick tock, tick tock. "You deceived me old man," she whimpered. "When I was young you passed by slowly. Oh, so terribly slowly. Now that I am old you are passing me by much too quickly."

"Have you not learned," said the old clock, "that I go neither slowly nor quickly? I cannot prolong the happy moments nor hasten the sad ones. I just go by."

"I know," the old queen sighed. "I know, my steadfast friend. In spite of all my attempts to rule over you as over my subjects, you were the one unyielding constant throughout my life."

"I am always here," the old grandfather clock said.

A tear came to the queen's eye. "But I am not."

The old clock tick tocked, tick tocked for a long time before he finally said, "You may join me if you wish."

The old queen still stooped over her cane raised her head and looked him in the face for the first time. Suddenly, her appearance changed. She straightened herself to full stature. She was regal and radiant. She took her place next to him in the middle of the room, her hands resting gently on the cane before her. The old grandfather chimed the hour, and when he was finished a new clock was added to that secret room in the castle tower.

~ 65 ~

Faithful Friend

"WILL YOU COME WITH ME, FRIEND? I am on a quest and I fear that I cannot make it all alone."

"Where are you going woman, and what can I do to help?" he asked.

"I am traveling to destiny, and the road is difficult and treacherous. But at the end of it I know there will be joy beyond measure and delight beyond all reckoning."

"Good woman, I have a road of my own to travel and a destiny of my own to pursue. Where will yours lead me and how far away will it take me?"

"Good sir, I know not where or how long it will take. Perhaps it is beyond the next hill or a year and a day away. I only know that I cannot make it without you."

So the man joined the woman and for a while they traveled. There were trials that bore heavily on them and difficulties beyond counting.

"Good woman," the man said. "Time is slipping past me and I fear for my own destiny. I will wither like the grass and my life pass like the wind with nothing to mark my being here because I sought not my destiny but yours."

"Faithful friend," the woman replied, "stay with me but a while longer for I feel that my destiny is close at hand. Then I shall accompany you to find yours."

And they traveled on. There was no respite. There was no comfort to solace them or friends to console them. There was only left to them the cold night and the distant stars. There wasn't even room for them in the Inn.

But God found them. And their destinies were not two but one. A child. At Bethlehem.

 Sugar and Salt

When sugar is added to food, it draws attention to itself.
When salt is added, it brings out the flavor of the food.
We are called to be the salt and not the sugar of the earth.

~ 66 ~

It's Christmas Night
and I'm Lonely

IT'S CHRISTMAS NIGHT and I'm lonely. I shouldn't be, I know, but I am. I feel so terribly alone and cut off. I feel as if I were a stone chip broken off a huge block of granite. Even if I were glued back on it would never be the same. You'd always see the line and be able to tell that I'm not really one with it anymore. I'm separate and distinct and I don't want to be. But there's nothing I can do about it. It's a fact of life whether I like it or not. I suppose that's what's making me feel so lonely this Christmas night.

I shouldn't feel lonely. I've traveled so far just to be here today. My folks were so happy to see me. I could feel it in the warmth of their hugs, especially, in my mother's kisses. They were so excited about seeing me. Strange, but that's exactly when I felt the first tinge of sadness. I wanted so bad to see them. Then when I did, I got this empty feeling in the pit of my stomach. Was it because if I hadn't seen them, I wouldn't have known how lonely I was? Seeing them, being with them only intensified the emptiness in me, in spite of their exuberance and joy. Yet, could I have stayed away? And on Christmas day?

The party was warm and wonderful. Maybe if it hadn't been I

wouldn't feel so unhappy later about what I'm missing. It's all very confusing. It's like saying I'd be better off having a terrible time so that I won't feel bad later. Then I'd feel bad earlier. Either way you can't win.

There's no reason for this loneliness. There were so many of us and we came from all over just to be here today. Is the rest of my family as lonely as I am or is it just me? They all seemed happy. I certainly felt good all day. There was so much talk and excitement that now that it's quiet and I'm alone I miss them. I'd miss them if I hadn't come and I miss them now that I've come and they're gone. It's just so confusing. All I know is that when everyone was around I didn't feel quite so lonely as I do now.

The wonderful presents I got helped. I could tell how much they enjoyed seeing the surprised look on my face over each new gift. I certainly delighted in the looks on their faces. That's what Christmas and gift giving is all about. The warmth of being together, of sharing and loving one another. The delight of Mom's good food, Dad's concern about making everyone feel comfortable, the children playing happily, the adults sharing stories — all these helped to fill the emptiness and satisfy the soul. It was a wonderful day. Truly, it was.

But with the night came parting. With the night came sorrow. Why couldn't the day have gone on? Why couldn't the feasting and the celebrating last forever, the way it should, the way it was meant to be? Why, Oh God, do I have to feel so lonely this Christmas night?

In the vast reaches of eternity the prayer is heard and God answers.

"Shhhh. Calm down and go to sleep, Jesus. This is just your first day on earth."

~ 67 ~

Harry Jordan

Harry Jordan was born wanting to get out. Everything was too confining for him. The womb may have been a warm and comfortable place to be, but he didn't remember it. He was never in any place long enough for him to remember. At least, that's the way he felt about life.

If there was a door, he had to open it. If there was a wall, he had to get over it. Freedom was always on the other side. It was always where he wasn't. But he was determined to get there.

The room he first found himself in was small, but it was infinitely bigger than the womb. Harry didn't just come out, he forced his way out. At least now there was room to breathe, a room to really move around in, which he did the moment he was able to.

At first, he crawled. That's when he discovered doors and hated them. Someone would have to open the door for him. No one did. He would have to stand up and do it himself. So he did.

The house, small as it was, was infinitely bigger than the room. There was upstairs and downstairs. There was an attic and a cellar and rooms in between. Here a body could roam.

That he did until he got to the front door. There was a world outside waiting for him, beckoning him. He waited for someone to open the door. But no one did. He would have to open it for himself, so he did.

There were no doors out there, just freedom. For the first time he could let his body move freely and his spirit soar mightily. There was nothing to confine him, no walls to surround him.

There was just a fence.

Of course, he had to get over it. And he did. He no longer waited for anyone to help him over it. He vaulted it by himself. The street was his. For as far as it went. Only it was a short street.

Harry Jordan went beyond the street into the tiny village of the town in the middle of nowhere, somewhere in middle America. He kept on walking past the door of the village and into the big city.

Here a man could stand full stature. He could wander far without walls or doors or picket fences. Farther than he had ever wandered before. This he did until he discovered that the city itself was a door that led to the country. No one would open this door for him. He had to do it himself. He hurried through it and the country stretched out before him.

But it was all for naught. The country was merely the door to the world. So, once again, he opened it and the world lay at his feet. But it didn't stayed beneath them for long. He walked, ran, sailed, and flew over it until he realized that the world was just another door. There was a universe out there waiting for him. Only then would he be truly free. Only out there would he be forever unconfined.

So in a space ship Harry Jordan was catapulted into the endless reaches of outer space to fulfill his life-long desire for freedom. He is out there, at this very moment. Somewhere in that unconfining infinity. He's been there for God knows how many years.

On rare occasions when they are able to make contact with him, they say that all he talks about is a small house on a short street in a tiny village in the middle of nowhere, somewhere in middle America.

~ Moral ~

Freedom is a door only God can open.

 ### The Egg Carton

*The egg carton was created, engineered, and crafted
to carry eggs . . . and not stones, jewelry, or buttons.
People were created, engineered, and crafted
for love . . . and not money, power, sex,
or any number of other things.
In both cases nothing else ever really fits.*

 ### Materialism

*Filling up your time with incessant activity
is just another form of materialism.*

~ 68 ~

Sandcastle

AN ARTIST wishing to entertain some children at a beach began to build them a sandcastle. The great prince of that land ventured by with some members of his court. When he saw what the artist was doing he marveled at his talent and workmanship.

"Who are you," the prince asked, "and what is it you do?"

"I am an artist and a sculptor," he replied. "What I am doing at present is building a house for myself that will have everything I have ever dreamed about. Then I take on little jobs here and there to support myself while I do my work. Why do you ask? Did you have something in mind?"

"I have harbored a desire these many years," the prince remarked, "to build an exemplary new capital city for our country since our present one is so old and run-down. Unfortunately, such an undertaking would be too time-consuming, especially since I would like it done in two years time when we shall be celebrating our sesquicentennial. Alas, I shall be hosting royalty from all over Europe for the event, but I have nothing to show them. It occurs to me that if you were to build me a magnificent model of what I propose to do, then when my guests come I will have not only something to show them but something that will awe them."

"Such an undertaking would take all of two years," said the artist "and I still have my own dream house to build."

"I will make it worth your while," the prince offered. "You will be provided with all you need. You can still work on your house in your spare time."

The artist agreed and immediately set about building a sandcastle. Because he wanted his work to be a credit to himself and the prince, he took meticulous care with every little bit of work he did. Such painstaking effort advanced the work slowly.

Each day the prince and his entourage would arrive and make constant recommendations and propose endless modifications. Nonetheless, the artist worked through it all with patience and care. The more alterations were offered the less and less time he had to himself and to work on his own house. Work on his own dream house diminished from part of the week, to two days a week, to one day a week, to one hour a week. There were weeks he did no work at all on it. What was once his sole objective was all but totally usurped by his preoccupation with building the sandcastle.

The prince had been true to his word. The artist never lacked for supplies or affirmation. Crowds gathered to applaud his work. Their numbers increased daily as they offered advice and accolades. A parapet was added here, more towers there. There was a moat and drawbridge. Houses and then a town itself were placed around the castle. A jousting field and amphitheater were added for sport and entertainment. The work got bigger and bigger until it stretched across the entire beach. In the end it was a monumental work of classic beauty, perfect symmetry, and good taste.

The day of celebration brought innumerable royalty and guests scurrying to see the masterpiece. Time, talent, and treasure had all been invested in this incomparable work. There was no end of praise for the artist and no small amount of accolades for the prince who commissioned it.

As the day drew to a close, a terrible storm loomed ominously over the horizon. Then came a violent wind followed by a torrential downpour. The sea lashed at the shore with a fury. The prince and his royal guests hurried off to the castle. The villagers returned to their own homes. The artist stayed behind desperately trying to protect his masterpiece. However, there was nothing he could do to stop the wind and the waves. Before long the sandcastle with its towers, moats, parapets, and houses melted back into the strand. There was nothing left for him to do but go home.

So long had it been since he had been there that he had forgotten how woefully unfinished it was. There was no roof and hardly any walls to speak of. What little of his dream house remained had fallen into disrepair.

The artist did not seek shelter from the storm. Instead, he deliberately sat on the unfinished floor of his incomplete hearth and let the rain wash over him throughout the night.

The next day, the artist set out once again with renewed fervor and conviction to build his dream house. From that day on until the day of his death he never again so much as thought of building another sandcastle.

~ Moral ~

The prince of this world commissions sandcastles.

 The One Who Has Everything
For the one who has everything,
to have nothing is gain.